# METROPOLIS

D0598151

MAN HAS
...NOW

A UNIVERSAL PICTURE

...time ago in a galaxy far, far away...

A STEVEN SPIELBERG FILM

# JURASSIC PARK

NO LONGER PROPERTY OF
ANYTHINK LIBRARIES/
RANGEVIEW LIBRARY DISTRICT

# THE
# SCIENCE
# FICTION
# UNIVERSE...
# AND BEYOND

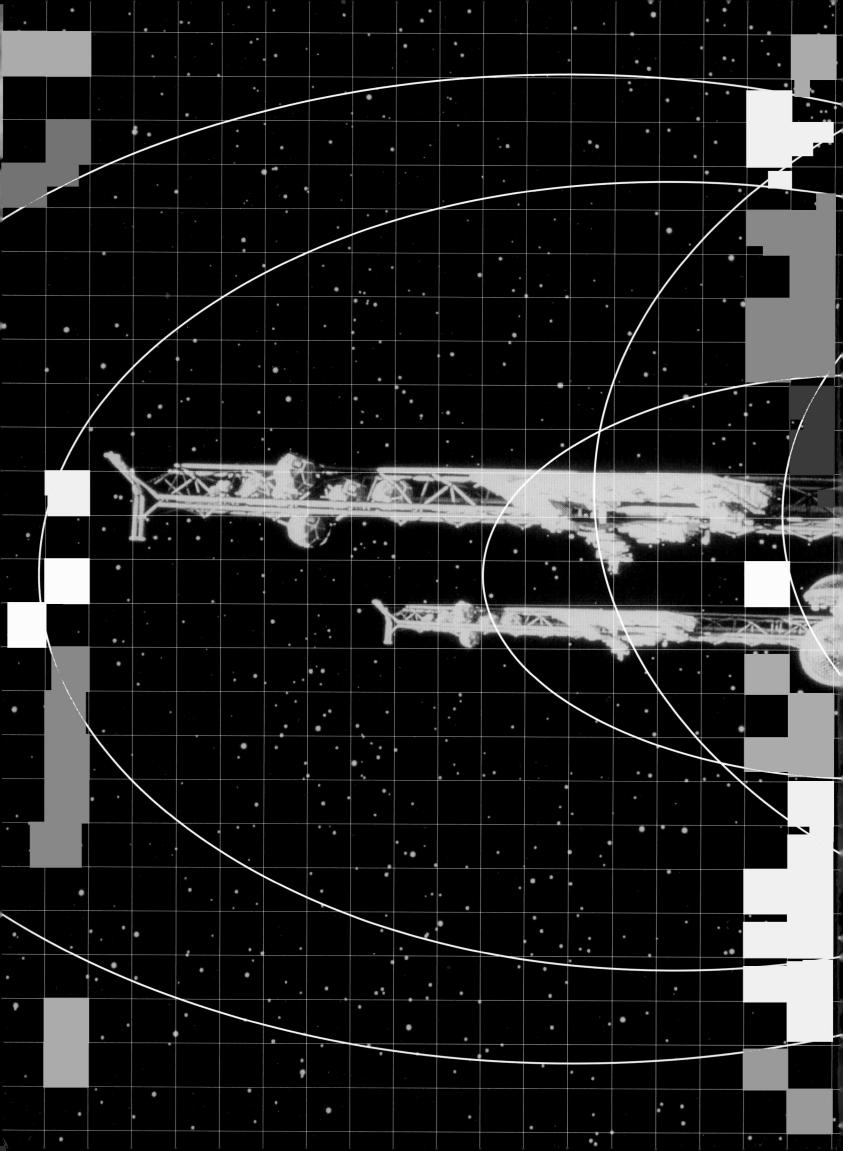

# THE SCIENCE FICTION UNIVERSE... AND BEYOND

## Syfy Channel Book of Sci-Fi

Introduction by Thomas P. Vitale, Syfy Channel
Text by Michael Mallory

UNIVERSE

First published in the United States of America in 2012
by Universe Publishing, A Division of Rizzoli International Publications, Inc.
300 Park Avenue South
New York, NY 10010
www.rizzoliusa.com

© 2012 Universal Television Networks

All rights reserved. No part of this publication may be reproduced, stored in a retrieval
system, or transmitted in any form or by any means, electronic, mechanical, photocopying,
recording, or otherwise, without prior consent of the publishers.

All images appear courtesy of Photofest and Syfy Channel.

Project Editors: Jim Muschett and Melissa Veronesi
Book Design: Chris McDonnell

ISBN 978-0-7893-2447-4
Library of Congress Catalog Control Number: 2012932100

2012 2013 2014 2015 / 10 9 8 7 6 5 4 3 2 1

Printed in China

# CONTENTS

# INTRODUCTION

**Introduction by Thomas P. Vitale,
Executive Vice President, Programming,
and Original Movies, Syfy**

Science fiction is important. In fact, I believe that sci-fi could be the most important genre in all of literature, television, and film. Through science fiction, every aspect of the human condition can be explored, just like in any other genre. But science fiction has the added benefit of stimulating the intellect and the imagination, while simultaneously providing visual, suspenseful, exciting, and moving entertainment. Over the years, science fiction has also become one of the most successful entertainment genres, with new movies, television series, and books sitting atop theatrical box office lists, Nielsen television ratings, and best-seller lists.

Yet, despite the success and popularity of science fiction (or maybe *because* of it), if you put any ten science fiction fans in a room, you'll get ten different definitions of what is and isn't science fiction. I'm a huge fan of the sci-fi genre, as well as related "imagination-based" genres, but I'm sure my personal definition of sci-fi won't completely agree with yours.

When Syfy sat down with the writer and publishers of the book you are holding, we spent hours debating what shows and movies should be covered in these pages and what would be left out. Was Superman an alien or a superhero? Should superheroes actually be covered in this book? Is Frankenstein science fiction—a creation of science—or a monster, chased by villagers with pitchforks? Is Ridley Scott's *Alien* a science fiction movie—a group of astronauts trapped in a small spaceship with an alien—or a horror movie—a group of disparate people trapped in a secluded location with a killer?

Many years ago at a sci-fi convention, a viewer of the network told me that *2001: A Space Odyssey* was the only "pure" science fiction movie ever made. All other space-based sci-fi movies featured explosions in space, which is scientifically inaccurate, since neither sound nor fire can exist in the vacuum of space, thus making all those other genre movies "sci-fantasy." This viewer said that *Star Trek* and *Star Wars* were "not really science fiction" according to his definition. He then told me that Syfy should only be in the business of airing "real science fiction." I smiled and said that if *2001* were truly the only "real" science

fiction movie ever made, then by that definition, we wouldn't have much to air on the network.

Of course, what we all enjoy watching, reading, writing, discussing, and imagining goes way beyond any question of "definition." We all enjoy many genres and types of entertainment. It all comes down to personal choices and everyone's choices are naturally different. But when programming a national television network, or choosing the content for a book, personal choices must be weighed against the preferences of the largest part of the audience. At Syfy, right from our first day back in September 1992, the decision was made to go beyond just science fiction, and also program fantasy, supernatural, horror, and related documentary and reality programming.

We decided to do this for a number of reasons. First, if we stuck with only "pure" science fiction, that sticky definition question would arise. Sure, most people define *Alien* as science fiction (though with a horror vibe), but what should we do with *Frankenstein*? Ultimately, while debating category and definition can be a fun and interesting way to pass some time, in the practical, daily world of creating and maintaining a television network, we must focus on providing a steady stream of quality entertainment to our viewers.

Through research with the general public, we've learned over the years that some people have the misperception that "science fiction" is *only* about space and aliens. Naturally, a major part of the world of science fiction is centered on stories about space and aliens, but real fans of the genre know that sci-fi also encompasses such areas as time travel, alternative history, future societies, imagined technologies, parallel dimensions, and so much more.

This is why, most importantly, Syfy is about the *imagination*. We invite our viewers to "imagine greater" and have decided that our programming should celebrate the wonder and power of imagination. Because of this philosophy, the scope of programming on Syfy can happily be fairly wide-ranging.

For example, our scripted series have run the gamut from the Peabody Award–winning *Battlestar Galactica*, to the fan-favorite *Farscape*, to the incredibly

**Above**: *Christopher Reeve as the best-known space alien in popular culture, Kal-El of Krypton, a.k.a. Superman.*

**Opposite**: *The "Star Child" from Stanley Kubrick's classic* 2001: A Space Odyssey.

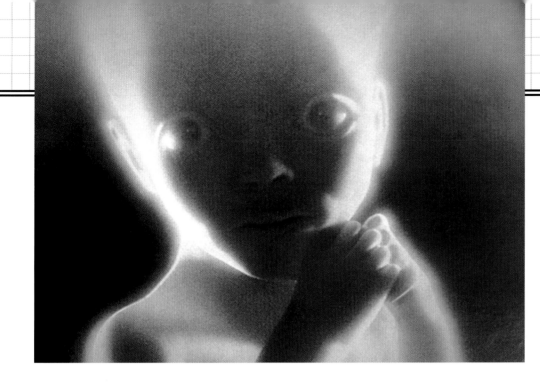

successful *Stargate* shows, to the comedy *Tripping the Rift*, to today's popular and imaginative series like *Eureka*, *Warehouse 13*, and *Alphas*, and so many more. In 2013, Syfy will be breaking new ground with a major new "transmedia" property, *Defiance*, which will simultaneously live as a dramatic television series as well as a major multi-platform, online game.

Syfy's scripted series have taken place in the past, the present, and the future. They have explored our world, alien worlds, parallel dimensions, politics, religion, science, family, and the human heart. Like all great storytelling, our shows are character based, but our characters reveal themselves in situations beyond those that we, the viewer, experience as reality in our own lives. Our characters experience their lives in the realm of the imagination.

In reality programming, we search for ghosts (*Ghost Hunters*), we hilariously prank friends and family via movie-inspired scenarios (*Scare Tactics*), and we watch amazing transformations happen right in front of our eyes (*Face Off*). These and other reality series on Syfy are also a celebration of the imagination. We are all seeking answers, and eternal questions such as what happens after death, speculative ruminations about the possibility of life on other worlds, and curiosity about how Hollywood magic is created are all ripe areas to explore.

In miniseries, we have adapted great books (Frank Herbert's *Dune*, *Legend of Earthsea*), explored some of the wondrous mysteries of our world (*The Triangle*), presented new takes on classic stories (*Tin Man*, *Alice*, *Neverland*) and have worked with legends, winning an Emmy in the process (*Steven Spielberg Presents Taken*).

Over the years, the various Syfy miniseries have been some of our most popular programs.

In documentaries, we have worked with archaeologists as they excavated the purported crash site of an alien ship at Roswell, New Mexico, sent respected journalist Lester Holt diving for evidence of anomalies in the Bermuda Triangle, and gathered experts to investigate the Mayan Calendar and the mystery behind the 2012 phenomenon. Going on such journeys to seek answers can be some of the best ways to ignite that imaginative spark that lives within all of us.

On Saturday nights, we invite our viewers to sit back, order a pizza, pop open a beverage of choice, and be entertained by our over-the-top take on the classic "drive-in" or "popcorn" movies. These imaginatively escapist movies range from pure science fiction, to creature features, to supernaturally driven horror, to disaster flicks (which we have dubbed "unnatural disasters"). Viewers have enjoyed more than two hundred of these Saturday original movies over the years, including *Sharktopus*, *Mansquito*, *Ice Twisters*, *Crimson Force*, *Cyclops*, *Swamp Volcano*, *Yeti*, *Alien Apocalypse*, *Pterodactyl*, and *Lake Placid 2* and *3*.

Rest assured that at Syfy, we also never forget the roots of science fiction and have happily been airing classic television series and movies alongside our more modern fare. Personal favorites of mine to present to viewers are Syfy's two annual *Twilight Zone* holiday marathons—one on New Year's Eve/Day and one on the Fourth of July. An argument can be made that *Twilight Zone* is the best television series ever made—not just the best science

fiction series, but the best *television* series overall. *Twilight Zone* was so far ahead of its time in dealing with an incredible range of important societal and human issues, and all within the context of gripping, imaginative storytelling. We hope you enjoy the *Twilight Zone* "spotlight" that you will find within these pages.

Finally, we also look for great imaginative programming from around the world to air on Syfy, whether it has been series like *Dr. Who* and *Merlin* out of the U.K. or *Lost Girl* from Canada, classic horror movies out of Italy, or famed monsters out of Japan. And the world looks back to Syfy for imaginative programming—in fact, Syfy is now operating in more than seventy territories around the globe, including parts of Latin America, Asia, and major European markets like France, the U.K., and Germany.

All this brings me back to the content of this book. While a television network has 365 days a year to try out different programming, adding, arranging, and (unfortunately) cancelling shows based on viewer reaction and popularity (usually, but not solely, measured by the Nielsen ratings), a book is a more finite object. If we were to try to include everything that Syfy is and will be—all the imaginative programming in the world—you would need a forklift to get this book home. Therefore, the focus of our text is geared towards *science fiction,* which is the core of Syfy. That doesn't mean that you will agree with our definition of sci-fi or with everything we've included, and I'm sure you will disagree with what we've excluded, but that's part of the fun. So, enjoy the text, photos, and art in the pages to follow, and let the debate begin!

CHAPTER 01

# EARLY DREAMS AND NIGHTMARES

**Above**: Georges Méliès at about the time his career in filmmaking began.

**Opposite**: Georges Méliès' original sketch of the Selenites, the moon creatures that appeared in A Trip to the Moon.

Science fiction has always seemed to be the most modern of any film genre, which is why it is startling to learn that it has been around for 110 years. Before the venerable western genre had been invented by Edwin S. Porter's *The Great Train Robbery* (1903), and even before heavier-than-air flight was proven to be a possibility by the Wright brothers, the cinema was taking audiences into outer space. The "astronaut" responsible for this was Parisian stage magician Georges Méliès, who saw possibilities in the nascent medium of the motion picture that no one else did.

### A Trip to the Moon
### (*Le Voyage dans la lune*)

Georges Méliès had become fascinated with motion pictures in the 1890s, and by accident discovered that film could be manipulated to illustrate fantasy—his camera jammed momentarily, and the resulting film seemed to show one passing object had suddenly transformed into another one. Using a combination of camera tricks and stage illusions, Méliès created a series of whimsical films with bizarre, fantastical elements. He had presented a voracious, Humpty Dumpty vision of the moon in the 1898 slapstick short titled *The Astronomer's Dream*, but Méliès is best remembered for his depiction of the first space flight in *A Trip to the Moon* (1902).

The fourteen-minute film (an epic for its day) depicts a group of astronomers, led by Professor Barbenfouillis, shooting themselves into outer space inside a bullet-shaped capsule fired from a cannon, a concept borrowed from Jules Verne's *From the Earth to the Moon* (1865). In one of the cinema's most famous images, the capsule splatters like a pie into the right eye of the Man in the Moon. Once there, the astronomers get caught in a snowstorm conjured up by the planet Saturn, which they escape by going underground. There they are besieged by the moon race of Selenites (a name borrowed from H. G. Wells's *The First Men in the Moon* [1901]), who when struck by the space travelers during a chase scene explode upon impact. After defeating the king of the Selenites, the astronomers return to Earth via freefall, where they land in the ocean and are towed to land and glory.

There are no title cards in the film, because it was originally accompanied by live narration. The film was also initially hand-colored frame by frame, giving audiences an even more striking visual experience. All hand-colored prints of the film were thought to be lost, since the negatives of most of Méliès's films had been rendered down to extract the chemicals in the film. But in 1993, a century after its production, a color print of *A Trip to the Moon* was discovered, in dire condition. Restoration of it began in 2002 and was not completed until 2010. It was screened at the Cannes Film Festival in 2011.

While the film is rudimentary by today's standards (and even by those of the 1930s), audiences of the time were thunderstruck and delighted by Méliès's ingenious special effects, which include double exposure and jump-cutting. Méliès might in fact be considered the James Cameron of his era (or perhaps the reverse is true), in that he was an *auteur*—not only writing, producing, and directing his films but designing and editing them

*Above: From* A Trip to the Moon, *the "space bullet" slamming into the face of the Man in the Moon has become one of the cinema's most iconic images.*

as well. He even plays Professor Barbenfouillis. Unfortunately, he became the first victim of the rough-and-tumble nature of the film industry. Rampant piracy of his films in America robbed him of income and forced him into bankruptcy in 1913. While Méliès was still highly regarded by many within the French film industry, he spent his later years selling toys in a train station to earn a living. In 2011, Méliès's story was again exposed to a broader audience, as Martin Scorsese's fantasy film *Hugo* features the older Méliès as a key character in the story.

### Metropolis
#### *"We shall build a tower that will reach the stars!"*

*Metropolis* (1927), director Fritz Lang's expressionistic masterpiece of class warfare in the world of 2026, took almost a year to shoot, between 1925 and 1926. Its imagery has become iconic: from its vision of an ultra-modern art deco city complete with aerial roadways, to its classic mad scientist's lab and the sight of hordes of workers shambling to and from their dehumanizing work shifts. It is, however, the sultry *Maschinenmensch*—the robot of *Metropolis*—that has become the signature image of the film.

Written by Thea von Harbou, who was then Lang's wife, *Metropolis* shows a world where the Managers, the privileged class, live and play aboveground in a modern Tower of Babel as the dehumanized workers toil underground. In the midst of this mechanical beehive, Freder (Gustav Frölich), the scion of Metropolis's founder, Joh Frederson, develops a social conscience through interaction with the beautiful Maria, who preaches to the workers that they need to wait for the coming of the Mediator, a messianic figure who will join the two classes together. Of course, Freder's destiny is to become the Mediator.

*Right*: An American release poster for Metropolis, highlighting the "Maschinenmensch," the film's central image.

*Left*: Fritz Lang (center) directs Brigitte Helm, as co-star Gustav Fröhlich (left) looks on in Metropolis.

**Above**: *Author H. G. Wells (left) visits actors Margaretta Scott and Raymond Massey on the set of* Things to Come.

**Opposite top**: *The dynamic creation scene of the "Machinenmensch" in* Metropolis *would influence later Frankenstein films.*

**Opposite bottom**: *The Tower from* Metropolis, *where the elite live.*

*Metropolis* contains a secondary plotline involving a mad inventor named Rotwang, who was a rival for the affections of Freder's late mother, and who creates a robot, eventually giving it the likeness of Maria. Eighteen-year-old Brigitte Helm played both Maria and the metallic Maschinenmensch. For the latter, Helm was encased in a form-fitting, hugely uncomfortable costume that was created by sculpting wood putty over a plaster cast of the actress and then covering it with metallic paint. (Lang later made up for it with a scene of the robotic Maria dancing in a club, for which Helm was encased in practically nothing.) To represent the towering city, effects cinematographer Eugen Schüfftan perfected a process that created the illusion of actors interacting with the fanciful sets by filming through a partially silvered mirror. The actors were visible through the plain glass part while the miniatures were reflected in the silvered part. The Schüfftan process became a staple of filmmaking.

When *Metropolis* premiered in 1927 it ran 153 minutes, but over the decades it has been cut by as much as half, with the Rotwang/Joh Frederson backstory and a subplot set in the city's red-light district eliminated. A restored 124-minute version was re-released in 2002, with still photos standing in for missing scenes. In 2008, a complete print was found in the Museo del Cine in Buenos Aires, and the original complete version was screened for the first time in eight decades at the 2011 Cannes Film Festival.

Director Fritz Lang would leave Germany a few years after making *Metropolis* to escape the rising Nazi party and settle in America (though his ex-wife, Thea von Harbou would remain behind). He resumed his directing career with a string of classic crime dramas and, more oddly, westerns, never again returning to science fiction.

### Things to Come
#### *"If we don't end war, war will end us."*

H. G. Wells was no fan of *Metropolis*. He trashed the film in an article published in the *New York Times*, in which he challenged Fritz Lang and Thea von Harbou's message that progress and automation had a dehumanizing effect on the masses. Wells presented his own vision of the future in 1933, in the novel *The Shape of Things to Come*, which postulated that the world would be torn apart by a prolonged war before finally settling into a new intellectual golden age. Three years later, he wrote the screenplay for the elaborate film version. It was produced by Alexander Korda and directed by William Cameron Menzies, then chiefly known as a film production designer.

*Things to Come* (1936) begins in 1940, when Everytown—a stand-in for London—is on the verge of war. Many choose not to believe war is coming, but some, such as John Cabal (Raymond Massey), fear that it is imminent. Cabal is right; war breaks out almost immediately and lasts for thirty years. By 1970, society has been reduced to a bombed-out, plague-decimated primitive existence under the control of the likes of the Boss, a

**Above**: *The older Cabal (Raymond Massey) surveys the carnage society has made of itself in* Things to Come.

**Opposite top**: *An elaborate view of a futuristic city in* Things to Come, *created through the "Schüfftan Process."*

**Opposite bottom**: *The unique design style of* Things to Come *combined futuristic and neoclassical looks.*

fur-clad, megalomanic warlord (Ralph Richardson). An older Cabal reappears, representing an airborne global unity force called Wings over the World, helps defeat the Boss and technology is once more on the march. By 2036, civilization has been fully rebuilt, and people live underground in fantastic, futuristic cities. A descendent of Cabal (also played by Massey) continues to preach the march of progress by advocating the conquest of space. He is opposed by an artist who sees the dark side of progress, named Theotocopulous (Cedric Hardwicke). Progress ultimately wins; the mobs that Theotocopulous has incited fail to destroy the space gun that blasts Cabal's daughter and her boyfriend into space, leaving Cabal to lecture on how man's destiny is to conquer the universe.

Things to Come could have been titled *Debate Over Things to Come*. Its philosophical speechifying did not appeal to all audiences of the time. But the highly detailed miniatures created by effects artist Ned Mann made an impact, particularly the scenes of the mobs storming the gigantic space gun, which were shot using the Schüfftan process. Wells's vision of the future was a return to the classical age, as discerned from the costumes in the future scenes that resemble Greek and Roman garb with a few Flash Gordon–esque flourishes.

**Above**: *Perhaps the quintessential B-Movie action star, Larry "Buster" Crabbe (top) not only played Flash Gordon but also Tarzan and Buck Rogers as well. His counterpart was Charles Middleton (above), seen here as the evil Ming the Merciless. Flash (Buster Crabbe) holds King Vultan ("Tiny" Lipson) at spearpoint to save Dale Arden (Jean Rogers) in* Flash Gordon *(top right).*

**Opposite**: *A miniature city of the future (1980, in context) from 1930's* Just Imagine, *from which some props and set pieces were borrowed for 1936's* Flash Gordon *(top). Max von Sydow channeled Charles Middleton as Ming in* Flash Gordon *(1980) (bottom left). Sam J. Jones channeled a store manikin as Flash in* Flash Gordon *(1980) (bottom right).*

### Flash Gordon
*"I will destroy your Earth in my own way."*

Movie serials—long, action-packed stories that played out in weekly fifteen-minute chapters—had been around since the 1910s, but by the mid-1930s they were entering their peak era. In 1936, Universal Pictures obtained the rights to *Flash Gordon*, Alex Raymond's popular newspaper comic strip, and set about to make a spectacle among serials. The budget was three times the norm for this sort of film, which the studio hoped would appeal to an adult audience as well as to kids. Despite the large budget, the film economically repurposed many of its sets and props, and even some footage from other Universal films, such as *The Mummy* and *The Bride of Frankenstein*.

The nominal plot of *Flash Gordon* involved Flash (Larry "Buster" Crabbe, an Olympic gold medalist in swimming), Professor Zarkov (Frank Shannon), and beautiful Dale Arden (Jean Rogers) traveling in Zarkov's spaceship to a mysterious planet called Mongo, which is on a collision course with Earth. There they find Mongo's dastardly ruler, Ming the Merciless (Charles Middleton), and spend the next twelve chapters fighting to keep him and his minions from destroying Earth.

A fifteen-chapter sequel titled *Flash Gordon's Trip to Mars*, featuring the creepy Clay People, followed in 1938, and a second sequel, *Flash Gordon Conquers the Universe*, featuring the Rock People, was released in 1940. Despite the studio hoopla over "spectacle," none of the miniature sets and flying spacecraft in any of the Flash Gordon serials scored better than adequate, but that was not really the point. With the exception of a bizarre, futuristic musical romantic comedy called *Just Imagine*, released by Fox in 1930, there were no other American-made sci-fi movies that ventured into space during the 1930s. There were plenty of mad doctors and monsters, but if you wanted a rocket ship, you had to go see Flash. In 1980, flamboyant Italian producer Dino De Laurentiis brought the character back to the big screen in an oversized, colorful adventure simply titled *Flash Gordon*. A beefy non-actor named Sam J. Jones (who had been discovered through an appearance on *The Dating Game*) was cast as Flash opposite Swedish actor Max von Sydow as Ming. While not very well received upon release, the film has aged well, and the soundtrack by the rock group Queen went on to become a modern (if campy) classic. Flash's last major outing was in a 2007 television series on Syfy, starring Eric Johnson as Flash. For this version of *Flash Gordon*, the characters eschew rockets and instead zoom to the planet Mongo through rifts in space.

*Right*: This is not a special effect; it is one of
the oversized sets built for Dr.Cyclops, with the
clapper-boy in the center.

*Right*: This is not a special effect; it is one of
the oversized sets built for Dr.Cyclops, with the
clapper-boy in the center.

*Below*: This is a special effect, with the "miniaturized" cast of Dr. Cyclops optically matted into a
shot with "giant" Albert Dekker.

*Opposite top*: A highly effective double-exposure
shot from Dr. Cyclops, combining the oversized
set with a regular-sized one.

*Opposite bottom*: Dr. Cyclops was the first sci-fi
film shot in three-strip Technicolor; 1955's This
Island Earth—which featured this ghastly
mutant—was the last.

## Dr. Cyclops
### "Strange how absorbed man has been in the size of things!"

There are no spaceships or future worlds to be found in Paramount's *Dr. Cyclops* (1940); rather, the movie covers ground established by *Island of the Lost Souls* (1933), which features a mad doctor in the jungle performing unholy experiments on people; *The Most Dangerous Game* (1932), in which a madman hunts human prey through a jungle; and even *King Kong* (1933), in which a group of people trail an enormous beast . . . in a jungle. The similarity between the latter two and *Dr. Cyclops* is no coincidence—all three films were directed (or co-directed) by Ernest B. Schoedsack, one of the lesser-remembered pioneers of sci-fi adventure.

Described by its studio as a "scientifilm," *Dr. Cyclops* concerns a myopic scientist named Thorkel (Albert Dekker), who invites fellow scientists to his jungle abode in Peru to help him with some work. Once there, they learn that he is perfecting a "radium-reducer ray" that will shrink organisms. When his visitors become too curious, Thorkel reduces them to the size of dolls and murders one, leaving the others to try and escape in the hostile jungle. The moniker "Dr. Cyclops" comes not only from the fact that Thorkel is the size of a monster, in comparison to his victims, but also because the tiny prisoners manage to shatter one lens in his Coke-bottle glasses, rendering him blind in one eye.

The illusion of disparity in size was accomplished through the use of oversized props and sets, rear projection using prefilmed backgrounds, and sometimes a combination of both. In one scene, Thorkel holds a miniaturized scientist in his hand; actor Charles Halton was positioned in the palm of an enormous, realistic prop hand that was perfectly aligned with the image of Dekker, who was rear-projected on a screen in the background. By the way, if the names Albert Dekker and Charles Halton don't ring any bells, that's because producer Dale van Every went out of his way to cast unfamiliar actors, thinking that this would further enhance the film's believability. "It naturally will be difficult to make audiences believe our characters have been reduced to a point where they are only twelve or fourteen inches high," he said in an interview at the time. "It would be impossible to make an audience believe it, for example, if we had Fred MacMurray and Barbara Stanwyck in the boy and girl roles. The public knows them too well." Given that *Dr. Cyclops* was filmed in 1939, though, its most marketable special effect was simply that it was shot in Technicolor, a first for any science fiction film. (For the record, the era of lush, three-strip Technicolor ended with a sci-fi picture, too: 1955's *This Island Earth*.)

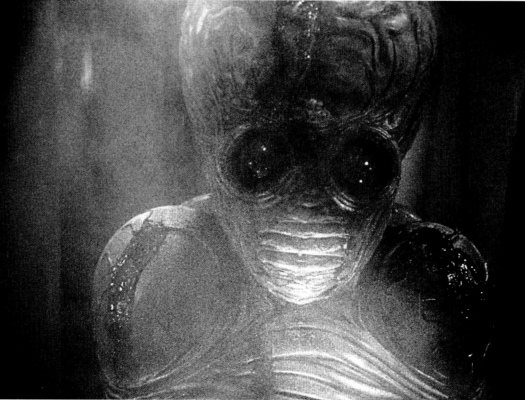

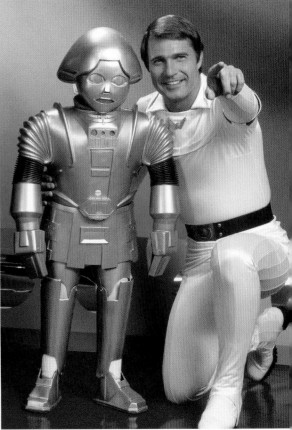

# "Thirteen episodes that will thrill you!"

They were fast—real fast. They were cheap—real cheap. And they were exciting. Serials catered to a mass audience and were meant to provide easy, escapist entertainment. Often featuring inferior actors, they were sometimes little more than excuses to stage nonstop chase scenes and fistfights, all leading up to a cliff-hanger chapter ending. But the cliff-hanger serials also kept science fiction alive in the 1930s and '40s. In fact, the first live-action appearance of Kal-El of Krypton came through the 1948 Columbia serial *Superman*, starring former dancer Kirk Alyn.

Given the popularity of Universal's *Flash Gordon* serials, the studio put Buster Crabbe through his paces again as *Buck Rogers* (1939), a twelve-chapter serial based on the popular comic strip about a modern man who Rip Van Winkles his way into the twenty-fifth century. Forty years later, Universal relaunched the property as the tongue-in-cheek NBC television series *Buck Rogers in the 25th Century*. It starred Gil Gerard as Buck and introduced into the mythology a *Star Wars*–style robot named

Twiki, voiced (in the first season and part of season two) by Mel Blanc, best known for doing the voice of Bugs Bunny and other classic cartoon characters, including animation's favorite comic alien, Marvin the Martian.

Other serials had sci-fi trappings, even if at heart they were crime dramas, such as Republic's *Fighting Devil Dogs* (1938), Universal's *The Phantom Creeps* (1939), starring Bela Lugosi as a mad scientist who controls a robot that looks like a tiki god, and Republic's *Mysterious Doctor Satan* (1940). But Republic's *The Purple Monster Strikes* (1945) features a genuine alien from the Red Planet, whose crash landing on Earth is discovered by a scientist. The man from Mars was played by a burly actor from westerns named Roy Barcroft, clad in a form-fitting outfit and medieval hood. Known only as the Purple Monster (though Barcroft himself enjoyed referring to the character as "the jerk in tights from Boyle Heights"), this alien is completely humanoid and has the ability to inhabit other people's bodies as well. Seemingly benign, his

Based on the SUPERMAN adventure feature appearing in SUPERMAN and ACTION COMICS magazines and in daily and Sunday newspapers coast to coast. Adapted from the SUPERMAN radio program.

with SUPERMAN · KIRK ALYN · LYLE TALBOT
NOEL NEILL · TOMMY BOND

Screen Play by GEORGE H. PLYMPTON, JOSEPH F. POLAND and DAVID MATHEWS

Directed by SPENCER BENNET · Produced by SAM KATZMAN · A COLUMBIA SERIAL

**Above**: *For the Superman serials, Superman was billed as playing himself (though Kirk Alyn, who actually played the role, is billed in small print).*

**Opposite left**: *Constance Moore, Buster Crabbe, and Jackie Moran were the stars of the Universal serial* Buck Rogers *(1939).*

**Opposite right**: *Gil Gerard as Buck with Twiki (Felix Silla inside the suit) in the television series* Buck Rogers in the 25th Century *(1979).*

ultimate goal is to launch a full-scale attack on Earth. A sequel of sorts was produced in 1950, titled *Flying Disc Man from Mars*. While it was not one of Republic's better serials, it introduced a theme that would recur throughout the 1950s: alien civilizations' concern that Earth people aren't ready to possess nuclear power.

1949's *King of the Rocket Men* introduced the earthly hero who wore a rocket pack that allowed him to fly. The hero also wore a bullet-shaped helmet that helped disguise the fact that it was stuntman David Sharpe doing the eye-popping dives and takeoffs, and not actor Tris Coffin, who played Jeff King (*King* of the Rocket Men . . . get it?). Republic Studio's special-effects wizards Howard and Theodore Lydecker further facilitated Rocket Man's flying scenes through the use of an oversized dummy

on wires, filmed against real backgrounds in natural lighting. The character (well, the costume at least) returned for 1952's *Radar Men from the Moon* and *Zombies of the Stratosphere*—in which Leonard Nimoy turned up as a Martian henchman—and *Commando Cody* (1953).

Serials diminished as television grew, and the kid-oriented sci-fi adventure that once dominated Saturday matinees were now the province of the small screen. *Captain Video and His Video Rangers*, which premiered on the DuMont network in 1949, featured the intrepid Captain Video (Richard Coogan, and then later Al Hodge), his Video Ranger (Don Hastings), and a robot labeled "Tobor"—because the prop crew had had the stencil flipped when they had sprayed the name on the costume. The live show featured scripts by some of

the top sci-fi writers of the day, including Jack Vance, James Blish, Robert Sheckly, C. M. Kornbluth, Walter M. Miller Jr., and even Arthur C. Clarke, and spawned a serial spin-off, Columbia's *Captain Video, Master of the Stratosphere* (1951), as well as the television imitations *Tom Corbett, Space Cadet* (1950), *Space Patrol* (1951), and *Rocky Jones, Space Ranger* (1954). The mid-1960s phenomenon *Batman* revived the spirit of the old chapterplays, offering two-part episodes with a cliff-hanger "ending" between them.

The era of the serials was gone by the 1970s, but they were not forgotten, at least not by George Lucas. The opening expository crawl at the beginning of *Star Wars* was a deliberate throwback to the science fiction serial of forty years earlier.

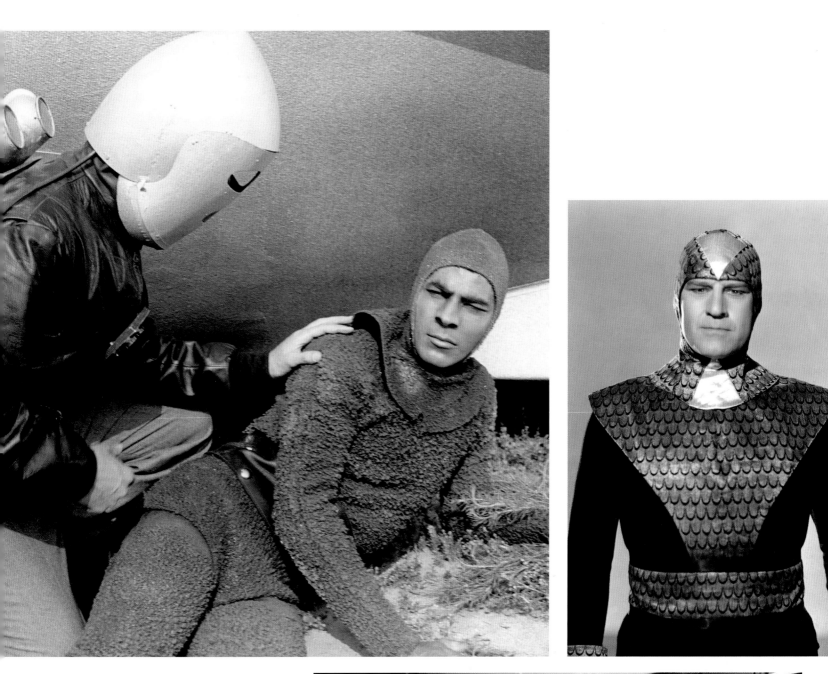

**Above**: With his hair and ears obscured, it is hard to recognize the actor playing the alien from 1952's Zombies of the Stratosphere: Leonard Nimoy.

**Above right**: Roy Barcroft as the mysterious Martian in The Purple Monster Strikes.

**Right**: Al Hodge and Don Hastings fend off the aliens in Captain Video.

**Opposite top**: Bela Lugosi (center), seen here examining actor Jack C. Smith, was the main attraction in the serial The Phantom Creeps.

**Opposite bottom**: 1949's King of the Rocket Men introduced the character Rocket Man, an inspiration for the later comic book and film The Rocketeer.

THE
FUTURE
IS
HERE!

ROCKETSHIP X-M

* EXPEDITION MOON

LLOYD BRIDGES · OSA MASSEN · JOHN EMERY
NOAH BEERY, JR. · HUGH O'BRIAN with MORRIS ANKRUM

Written and Directed by KURT NEUMANN · Director of Photography KARL STRUSS, A.S.C.
Executive Producer MURRAY LERNER · Released by LIPPERT PICTURES, Inc.

02

The he end of World War II did not simply have an enormous effect on the world from a societal standpoint; it also greatly affected the shape of entertainment. During this time the western became less about shootouts and chase scenes and more about human drama in situations of struggle and hardship, and mystery films graduated from being lighthearted whodunits and capers to film noir crime dramas that meant business. Prior to and during the war, science fiction movies were primarily fantasy adventure for kids, with a lot more emphasis on the *fiction* than the *science*. After the war, people began to speculate more seriously about the possibility of spacecraft and what the crews of those spacecraft might find elsewhere in the universe. In the 1950s, sci-fi grew up—and outward.

### Destination Moon

#### *"It'll never get off the ground . . . no propellers!"*

Art imitated life in 1950, as a second space race heated up between two movies vying to be the first off the launchpad to present a manned flight to the moon, *Rocketship X-M* and *Destination Moon*. The much-lower-budget *Rocketship X-M*, legally blocked from using its original title, *Expedition Moon* (hence *X-M*), was rushed into production by ultra-indie Lippert Productions to beat *Destination Moon* to theaters. It did, by a few weeks, but *Destination Moon* had the far greater impact.

Released by Eagle-Lion Classics, a small studio that was formed out of the ashes of PRC, the most poverty-stricken of Hollywood's Poverty Row studios, *Destination Moon* offered a serious look at the first manned spaceflight and its mission's goal of landing on the surface of the moon before the Russians. The Reds, however, remain in the background of the plot. *Destination Moon* begins with a debate between the scientists who have secured private funding for the venture and are convinced that the rocket will succeed, and the skeptics who do not. The debate continues even after the rocket takes off from the New Mexico desert and lands on the moon's surface, because the four-man crew (played by a no-star cast) discovers they may lack sufficient fuel to return home.

*Destination Moon* took its special effects very seriously. A large model rocket was built, as was a soundstage-filling moonscape designed by Chesley Bonestell, an artist renowned for his speculative paintings of other worlds that appeared in popular magazines. The set of the moon utilized a twenty-foot-tall cyclorama based on a two-by-twenty-foot painting by Bonestell, along with a set representing the moon's surface (though Bonestell's cracked, dried-mud interpretation would prove inaccurate). For shots of endless space, backdrops of black velvet were hung, as were some two thousand light bulbs in varying sizes representing stars and other celestial bodies. One of the most startling effects was the rocket ship crew experiencing extreme g-forces on takeoff. Thin, almost invisible strips of membrane were attached to the actors' faces and then pulled in various directions, supplying the illusion of the force of gravity distorting their features. The special effects, supervised by Lee Zavitz, won an Oscar.

**Above**: *The outer space sequences for* Destination Moon *were based on space artist Chesley Bonestell's paintings.*

**Opposite top**: *Warner Anderson and John Archer in* Destination Moon.

**Opposite bottom**: Rocketship X-M *raced* Destination Moon *to theaters in 1950, but was not allowed to use its original title,* Expedition Moon, *because of the similarities.*

FROM OUT OF SPACE.....
A WARNING AND AN ULTIMATUM!

THE
DAY
THE
EARTH
STOOD
STILL

WITH
**MICHAEL RENNIE · PATRICIA NEAL · HUGH MARLOWE**
SAM JAFFE · BILLY GRAY · FRANCES BAVIER · LOCK MARTIN
PRODUCED BY JULIAN BLAUSTEIN · DIRECTED BY ROBERT WISE · SCREEN PLAY BY EDMUND H. NORTH  20th CENTURY-FOX

*Destination Moon* was based on the novel *Rocketship Galileo*, by Robert A. Heinlein, who co-wrote the screenplay with Alford "Rip" Van Ronkel and James O'Hanlon. It was the first science fiction picture produced by George Pal, who would become a major force in the genre throughout the 1950s. Prior to *Destination Moon*, the Hungarian-born Pal was best known as the producer of *Puppetoons*, a series of stop-motion-animated cartoons featuring wooden doll-like characters with interchangeable heads. (A young Ray Harryhausen got his start in the *Puppetoon* series.) The only moment of whimsical fantasy in the film came through an animated cameo appearance by Woody Woodpecker, who shows up in a simulated tutorial explaining the finer points of space travel. The cartoon was later reworked and promoted by NASA.

*Above*: The actual film The Day the Earth Stood Still *was a little more thoughtful than this melodramatic poster would make it appear.*

*Above right*: Hungarian-born George Pal (1908–80) was a major figure in the development of science fiction in the cinema.

**The Day the Earth Stood Still**
*"If you threaten to extend your violence, this Earth of yours will be reduced to a burnt-out cinder."*

No sooner had we launched outward to explore space on film than those living in outer space showed up to confront us. *The Day the Earth Stood Still* (1951) depicts the arrival of a flying saucer—a term that had been popularized in the press in the late 1940s—in Washington, D.C. An alien named Klaatu (Michael Rennie) emerges from the spaceship and announces that he comes in peace and with goodwill. The military forces that have surrounded the ship shoot first and ask questions later. With Klaatu lying injured, another alien appears: an eight-foot-tall robot named Gort, who has a built-in disintegrator ray in his head. Klaatu is taken into custody, where he reveals he has a message for the world leaders, who are more interested in fighting each other than listening to an alien. Assuming the guise of a soldier named Carpenter, Klaatu escapes the military facility and infiltrates society, striking up a friendship with a woman named Helen (Patricia Neal) and her son Bobby (Billy Gray).

*Above*: The massive robot Gort (Lock Martin) emerges from the spaceship in The Day the Earth Stood Still.

Eventually Klaatu reveals his message for the people of the Earth: if the world's leaders do not cease their nuclear aggression, then they risk extermination by the forces of other planets. To demonstrate his power, Klaatu causes a global electrical power outage for one half hour, which brings Earth to the standstill of the title. Tensions heat up to the point where Klaatu tells Helen that, should something happen to him, she needs to go to Gort, speak the phrase "Klaatu barada nikto," and Gort will understand and call off the attack on Earth. Klaatu is shot, but the giant sentry pulls him into the ship, which takes off.

Filmed under the much more prosaic title *Journey to the Earth*, *The Day the Earth Stood Still* was directed by Robert Wise, whose long Hollywood résumé covers virtually every film genre there is, from horror (*The Body Snatchers*) to musicals (*The Sound of Music*). Many commentators at the time noticed not only the social message in Edmund H. North's script but its religious overtones. Klaatu's mission is to save the Earth from itself; and he dies and is resurrected in order for his message of "love thy neighbor" to sink in. And if that isn't obvious enough for viewers, his human persona's name is "Carpenter"— Jesus's profession. Moreover, the casting of placid, ascetic Michael Rennie was interpreted as the filmmakers' going for a definite Christ-like image. Officially though, the English actor was cast because he was unknown to American audiences and had an unusual voice that seemed to carry all accents yet no specific one.

The robot Gort was played by seven-foot-seven-inch Lock Martin, who not surprisingly specialized in giant roles (he also played a Martian mutant in 1953's *Invaders from Mars*). His costume was made of foam rubber molded over a frame of fiberglass cloth that was

**Above**: The orb-like spacecraft from the 2008 remake of The Day the Earth Stood Still.

**Left**: Klaatu (Keanu Reeves) undergoes testing in 2008's The Day the Earth Stood Still.

**Opposite**: Klaatu (Michael Rennie, waving) comes in peace, or at least tries to, in 1951's The Day the Earth Stood Still.

painted silver. There were two different versions of the costume: one with an opening in the front and one with an opening in the back. Usage depended on how Martin was positioned in front of the camera. The film's one-hundred-foot-by-twenty-five-foot spaceship was designed by art directors Lyle Wheeler and Addison Hehr. They added a clever touch to the scenes in which its portals opened: the seams of the closed doors were covered with plastic and painted so as to look solid, enhancing the surprise when an opening suddenly appeared.

*The Day the Earth Stood Still* was remade in 2008 with Keanu Reeves as Klaatu, while Gort gained twenty feet in height and was created with digital animation. In this version, Klaatu delivers an ecological message, telling the people of Earth that they must stop trashing their little corner of the universe . . . or else. Ultimately, Klaatu becomes convinced humankind is worth saving and sacrifices himself to do so. At Reeves's insistence, the phrase "Klaatu barada nikto" was reused; but, as was the case in the original film, the phrase is never fully explained.

## The Thing from Another World
### *"Keep watching the skies."*

*The Thing from Another World* (1951) was as influential as *The Day the Earth Stood Still* in establishing what would become standard sci-fi themes and character dynamics. Set on a U.S. Air Force outpost in the Arctic, *The Thing from Another World* is equal parts horror film and science fiction picture. There is a spaceship and an alien, which is chipped out of the permafrost by the airmen and revived; but once that is out of the way, *The Thing* (as it is commonly known) becomes a monster movie.

*Above: James Arness as the title creature of* The Thing from Another World *is shown here with much more clarity than is ever seen in the film itself.*

*Opposite top: The discovery of the creature in ice from* The Thing from Another World. *The actor at far right is voice artist Paul Frees, making a rare on-camera appearance.*

*Opposite bottom: The non-star cast of* The Thing from Another World *included George Fenneman—Groucho Marx's cohort on* You Bet Your Life—*Robert Cornthwaite, Margaret Sheridan, and Kenneth Tobey.*

Produced and supervised, if not actually directed, by Howard Hawks—his regular editor Christian Nyby is credited as director, but the debate over who actually called the shots rages to this day—*The Thing* pioneered two key sci-fi movie concepts: one being the plot of a team stranded in some remote location and threatened by an alien force; the other being the theme of the ongoing conflict between military mentality (*Let's kill it!*) and scientific mentality (*Let's communicate with it to understand it.*). In this film, the fact that the alien is clad in what resembles a utilitarian, Communist-style work suit clued in Cold War audiences as to which side they should root for.

As was becoming the norm for sci-fi films, Hawks deliberately cast the picture with solid but unfamiliar actors, including Kenneth Tobey, Margaret Sheridan, and Robert Cornthwaite. The most unfamiliar (and unrecognizable) of all was the actor playing the Thing, six-foot-seven-inch James Arness, three years away from picking up his badge on television's *Gunsmoke*. Seeking realism, the film's producer Edward Lasker submitted the script to the U.S. Air Force in order to obtain military cooperation. He was unsuccessful, and quoted the reply from the Air Force as: "We've spent half a million dollars proving there are no such things as flying saucers. Why should we help you make a picture about one?"

For decades, the film was known simply as *The Thing*. Even reviewers of the time could not decide whether the official title was *The Thing* or *The Thing from Another World*. Why the confusion? While the film was in production in 1950, a novelty song called "The Thing," composed by Charles Randolph Grean, became a surprise hit, even reaching number one on the charts. Because Hawks did not want his very serious film mistaken for a goofy Hit Parade song, he added "*from Another World*" to the title at the last minute.

John Carpenter's 1982 remake of *The Thing* adhered more closely to the original source material, John W. Campbell Jr's., short story *Who Goes There?*. Carpenter's alien was not a big, ugly Frankensteinian monster but an organism that could transform into the image of anything living. Kurt Russell starred as the leader of the isolated Antarctic research expedition that is forced to combat the alien life force, which has already

**Above**: *Kurt Russell realizes something isn't right in John Carpenter's 1982 remake of* The Thing.

**Right**: *It's not Frankenstein's Monster being brought to life; it's the Thing (James Arness) being zapped to death in* The Thing from Another World.

The ultimate in alien terror.

JOHN CARPENTER'S

THE THING

A TURMAN-FOSTER COMPANY PRODUCTION JOHN CARPENTER'S 'THE THING'

STARRING KURT RUSSELL SCREENPLAY BY BILL LANCASTER SPECIAL VISUAL EFFECTS BY ALBERT WHITLOCK SPECIAL MAKE-UP EFFECTS BY ROB BOTTIN MUSIC BY ENNIO MORRICONE DIRECTOR OF PHOTOGRAPHY DEAN CUNDEY ASSOCIATE PRODUCER LARRY FRANCO

R RESTRICTED EXECUTIVE PRODUCER WILBUR STARK CO-PRODUCER STUART COHEN PRODUCED BY DAVID FOSTER & LAWRENCE TURMAN DIRECTED BY JOHN CARPENTER A UNIVERSAL PICTURE ©1982 UNIVERSAL CITY STUDIOS, INC.

SOUNDTRACK AVAILABLE ON MCA RECORDS & TAPES BASED ON THE STORY "WHO GOES THERE?" BY JOHN W. CAMPBELL, JR. READ THE BANTAM BOOK PANAVISION® DD DOLBY STEREO IN SELECTED THEATRES

decimated a nearby Norwegian camp. Once it is discovered that the parasitic alien life force is capable of taking over the bodies of the expedition members, the rest of the crew is forced to figure out who is still human and who is not.

Not only was the paranoia factor ratcheted up in this version of *The Thing*; the film also raised the cinematic bar on the "ick" factor, with bloody, juicy, head-and-body-splitting special effects, courtesy of Rob Bottin. Moviegoers and reviewers of the time were not accustomed to seeing such graphically gory images (critic Roger Ebert dubbed it "a great barf-bag movie"), and as a result some were repulsed. The film was not a success upon release, suffering at the time from comparisons with both the original, which by then had achieved classic status, and the much warmer *E.T. the Extra-Terrestrial*, which was released two weeks prior to it. Time has allowed it to be accepted on its own merits and appreciation has grown for the film and its pioneering special effects. Like Hawks's original, Carpenter's *The Thing* is now regarded as a sci-fi/horror classic.

The story got a third go-around in 2011, once again titled *The Thing*. Presented as a prequel to the 1982 film, this version chronicled a joint American and Norwegian research team that discovers the body of an alien creature in a wrecked spacecraft, unaware that it is still alive.

*Above*: *While John Carpenter's* The Thing *was not well received upon release in 1982, its reputation has grown in the years since.*

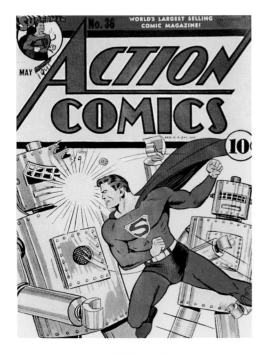

*Above top: Kal-El of Krypton, a.k.a. Superman, started putting the action in "Action Comics" in 1938. He is seen here on the cover of the May 1941 issue.*

*Above right: Superman as seen in the Max Fleischer animated cartoons, produced in 1941 and 1942.*

*Above: Radio actor Clayton "Bud" Collyer was the voice of Clark Kent/Superman for the radio series and the cartoons.*

### Adventures of Superman
*"A never-ending battle for truth, justice, and the American way!"*

When two young men named Jerry Siegel and Joe Shuster created a character called Superman in the mid-1930s, they had no idea he would go on to become the most famous space alien of the twentieth century. After his comic book debut in 1938, Superman became a radio star in 1940 and, starting the following year, was seen in a series of short cartoons produced by Max Fleischer, which were unique as the only dramatic cartoon shorts of the golden age of animation, from the late 1930s through the 1950s. Superman and his alter ego, Clark Kent, first appeared in live action in the 1948 serial *Superman* and its sequel, 1950's *Atom Man vs. Superman*. In both, Kirk Alyn played Kent and Superman uncredited, to enable the fiction that the producers had hired the "real" Man of Steel. But it is the television series starring George Reeves, one of the most successful syndicated series of all time, that people remember best.

Reeves first donned Superman's cape and Clark's eyeglasses in a very low-budget feature film titled *Superman and the Mole-Men* (1951), which served as the pilot for *Adventures of Superman*. The series's first episode, "Superman on Earth" (1952) tells of how baby Kal-El of the planet Krypton is rocketed to Earth by his scientist father, Jor-El, right before Krypton faces destruction. The infant is found and taken in by Eben and Sarah Kent (not Jonathan and Martha, as they are usually named), and raised to young adulthood, at which point he moves to the teeming city of Metropolis and begins his heroic career. Initially, Superman's launches into the air were accomplished by having Reeves pulled aloft on wires, but while they were filming the episode "Ghost Wolf" in 1952, the wires broke and Reeves landed in a heap. He was not seriously hurt, but subsequent takeoffs were staged by having Reeves jump on a springboard and dive out of camera range.

Unlike Kirk Alyn and Bud Collyer, who voiced the character both on radio and for the cartoons, Reeves made virtually no distinction between the characters of Superman and Clark Kent, but still became so identified with the role that he had trouble finding other work. *Adventures of Superman* ceased production in 1957 and left the airwaves the following year. In June 1959, the forty-five-year-old Reeves was found dead from a gunshot wound in the bedroom of his home. His death was ruled a suicide, and it was assumed that despondency about being typecast was the motivation. An alternative theory that Reeves might instead have been murdered has gained traction over the years.

In 1978, the character returned to the big screen in the big-budget *Superman*. Kal-El's Kryptonian backstory was dramatized as never before, and Marlon Brando featured prominently as Jor-El. Twenty-four-year-old Christopher Reeve became an instant star in the lead role(s), and the special effects, supervised by Colin Chilvers, Roy Field, Derek Meddings, and Les Bowie, included highly convincing flying scenes, accomplished with wire work. Reeve appeared in three more sequels: *Superman II* (1981), *Superman III* (1983), and *Superman IV: The Quest for Peace* (1987), and actually managed to escape being typecast. In 1995 he suffered a serious equestrian accident that left him quadriplegic. Continuing to act and direct from an automated wheelchair, Reeve became an activist for the disabled until his death in 2004.

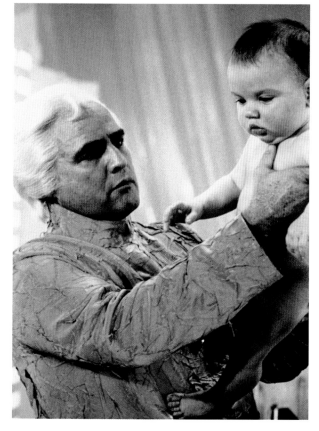

**Top left**: *Jack Larson, John Hamilton, Noel Neill, and George Reeves were the longtime cast of TV's* Adventures of Superman.

**Top right**: *Noel Neill and George Reeves pose while filming* Adventures of Superman.

**Middle left**: *Phyllis Coates as Lois Lane hides behind George Reeves as he faces angry villager Jeff Corey in the feature film/television pilot,* Superman and the Mole Men *(1951).*

**Bottom left**: *Jor-El (Marlon Brando) makes his son an offer he can't refuse—sending him to Earth—in 1978's* Superman.

**Bottom right**: *Christopher Reeve soaring high in* Superman.

*Top*: Teri Hatcher and Dean Cain in Lois & Clark: The New Adventures of Superman.

*Above*: Brandon Routh brings down the house—slowly—in Superman Returns.

*Right*: Tom Welling takes a noirpunk stance as the Man of Steel in television's Smallville.

Superman kept flying on television. The 1993 ABC series *Lois & Clark: The New Adventures of Superman* concentrated as much on the relationship between Clark and Lois as it did on adventure; and the WB Television Network's *Smallville*, which premiered in 2001, injected some teen angst into the already complicated life of young Clark Kent. The saga was rebooted for the big screen in 2006 with *Superman Returns*, which starred Brandon Routh as Superman/Clark. Having more of a sci-fi element than the previous films, it depicted Superman traveling to space to try and find the remnants of his destroyed planet. While high-tech digital effects replaced the old techniques of flying on wires or optical compositing into a scene, Superman himself remained as powerful as ever. The next Superman movie, *Man of Steel*, will star Henry Cavill as the titular character and is slated for release in 2013.

### The War of the Worlds
**"We know now we can't beat their machines. We've got to beat them!"**
After producing *Destination Moon*, George Pal turned to a more fanciful theme with *When Worlds Collide* (1951). This film established the global-destruction subgenre of sci-fi in a tale about a newly discovered star passing close enough to the Earth to destroy it, forcing a group of earthlings to blast off to another inhabitable planet in hopes of preserving the species. His next project, a lavish, updated version of H. G. Wells's *The War of the Worlds* (1953), would become one of his biggest successes.

**Above**: *Orson Welles (left, arms upraised) rehearsing the October 30, 1938, radio broadcast of* The War of the Worlds. *At right is William Alland, who would later produce such sci-fi classics as* It Came from Outer Space.

*Opposite top*: *A special effects technician rigs one of the Martian craft for a shot on a miniature set in 1953's* The War of the Worlds.

*Opposite bottom*: *The Martian attack as it appears on film in* The War of the Worlds.

*Top*: *One of the Oscar-winning special effects from 1951's* When Worlds Collide.

*Above left*: *Gene Barry and Ann Robinson were the terrestrial stars of* The War of the Worlds.

*Above right*: *Producer George Pal (left) consults with director Byron Haskin on the set of* The War of the Worlds (1951).

*The War of the Worlds* already had a place in entertainment history: on the evening of October 30, 1938, a radio dramatization of the story by Orson Welles, done in the format of a series of news bulletins, caused a panic among listeners who thought the country was really being invaded by aliens. Pal's film version, directed by Byron Haskin (who, prior to launching a directing career, had been the head of the special-effects department at Warner Bros.), was set in and around Los Angeles, though it is made clear that the Martians are landing all over the world. The aliens waste little time in going on the attack, shooting destructive beams from war machines that resemble flying manta rays with Loch Ness Monster necks. At first, the earthlings are powerless against them; even an atomic bomb doesn't slow them down. What *does* finally defeat the Martians is a simple earthly virus, which infects and kills the beings inside the war machines. In the film's final moments, God is given the credit for Earth's survival.

While actors Gene Barry and Ann Robinson were the official stars of the film, most of the attention was directed toward the special effects—nearly three-quarters of the film's $2 million budget. A lot of the effects, which took some six months to complete, entailed filming miniature sets and model spaceships, with special-effects supervisor Gordon Jennings building on what his team had done in *When Worlds Collide* (a film that had won

him an Oscar for Special Effects). One of the picture's most iconic scenes, the Los Angeles City Hall being blasted to pieces by Martian marauders, involved blowing up a detailed six-foot-high model of the building. Three models of the Martian pod craft were created, each forty-two inches in diameter and supported by wires (which are on occasion very visible on camera). To simulate the atomic bomb dropped on the Martian craft, a pile of colored flash powder was detonated and filmed at three times the normal speed so that the actual blast would appear slow on the film. The actual organic Martian resembled a short, stunted tree with tricolor lenses for an eye. The costume was built out of rubber and papier-mâché and played by an actor/costumer/makeup artist named Charles Gemorah, who was known in Hollywood for playing gorillas.

In addition to winning yet another special-effects Oscar, *The War of the Worlds* has another lasting legacy: Gene Barry's character is named Dr. Clayton Forrester, which years later was the name of the mad scientist in the comedy television series *Mystery Science Theater 3000*.

Steven Spielberg's epic 2005 remake of the story, *War of the Worlds* (no "*The*"), generally followed the accepted storyline, though now the Martian war machines were the tripodal, towerlike vehicles described by Wells in the novel rather than the manta-ray-style hovering craft. In an effort to heighten the realism, practical sets and effects were used as much as possible, frequently augmented by computer-generated imagery. The most spectacular set was one depicting the result of a Boeing 747 jetliner crashing into a residential neighborhood. That enormous set is still intact, and is now an attraction on the Universal Studios Tour in Hollywood.

**Above**: *A Martian war machine on the attack in Steven Spielberg's 2005 remake of* War of the Worlds.

**Opposite**: *One of the Martians outside of their protective craft, from 1953's* The War of the Worlds.

# *"Take your stinking paws off me, you damned, dirty ape!"*

These days, *Planet of the Apes* might be seen as the film that launched a thousand clichés and catchphrases, most of them involving star Charlton Heston's thundering delivery of his dialogue ("It's a madhouse . . . a maaadhouuuuse!"). But when the film was first released in 1968, it was greeted with a great deal of serious attention, most of it for its obvious attraction: the innovative, brilliant makeup work supervised by John Chambers, which turned a large cast of actors into highly believable talking gorillas, chimps, and orangutans. But there was, and is, much more to *Planet of the Apes* than state-of-the-art prosthetics.

Scripted by Rod Serling of *Twilight Zone* fame and Michael Wilson (who rewrote Serling's original screenplay) and based on the 1963 sci-fi novel *Monkey Planet* by French author Pierre Boulle, and directed by Franklin J. Schaffner, *Planet of the Apes* was a confluence of many established sci-fi themes: the military vs. science, paranoia, space travel, time travel, and ultimately, trepidation about nuclear technology. The film's now-iconic ending—in which astronaut Taylor (Heston) realizes the "alien" planet onto which he has crash-landed is a future Earth where apes are in charge and humans are unevolved slaves—was a genuine shocker at the time.

Understanding that if the apes did not work, the film would not work, producer Arthur P. Jacobs dedicated approximately one-tenth of the film's $6 million budget

**Above**: Charlton Heston (center) is judged by a jury of his . . . peers? . . . in Planet of the Apes.

**Opposite**: The ape village for Planet of the Apes was actually built in the Santa Monica Mountains of Malibu.

to makeup and raided every film set in Los Angeles for talent to build the army of makeup artists—upwards of eighty on some days—necessary for the shoot. *Planet*'s spaceship sequences were filmed at Lake Powell, Utah, whose rugged terrain looked arguably alien. The strange, primitive ape village was built at the 20th Century Fox ranch in Malibu Canyon.

In the 1970 sequel *Beneath the Planet of the Apes*, written by Paul Dehn and directed by Ted Post, a new astronaut named Brent (James Franciscus) crash-lands on the same planet, intent on learning what happened to Taylor. He does, but prior to that he encounters the slave woman Nova (Linda Harrison), whom Taylor had befriended in the first film, and a race of radiation-burned human telepaths living underground in the ruins of twentieth-century New York, where they worship the bomb that destroyed their city. The massive sets of a decimated New York were impressive (though actual Big Apple moviegoers were probably surprised to

see all their city's landmarks located next to one another), but at times the film plays like a strange, dark satire, particularly in the atonal hymns that the humans sing to their bomb.

The next entry, *Escape from the Planet of the Apes* (1971), swung back to being a serious, realistic social drama. Two of the series' lead apes, Dr. Zira (Kim Hunter) and Cornelius (Roddy McDowall), manage to repair the spaceship abandoned by Taylor in the first film and take off in it, arriving back on Earth in modern times (which saved a great deal in makeup costs). The public adopts them, but the government fears them, particularly after Zira reveals she is pregnant. When the feds learn that apes have overtaken humans in the future, treated them like slaves, and used them for medical research, they believe they can change the future by forcing Zira to abort her child. Zira and Cornelius flee and Zira gives birth, but the fugitive apes are hunted down by the military and killed. So, it appears, is the baby. But Zira switched

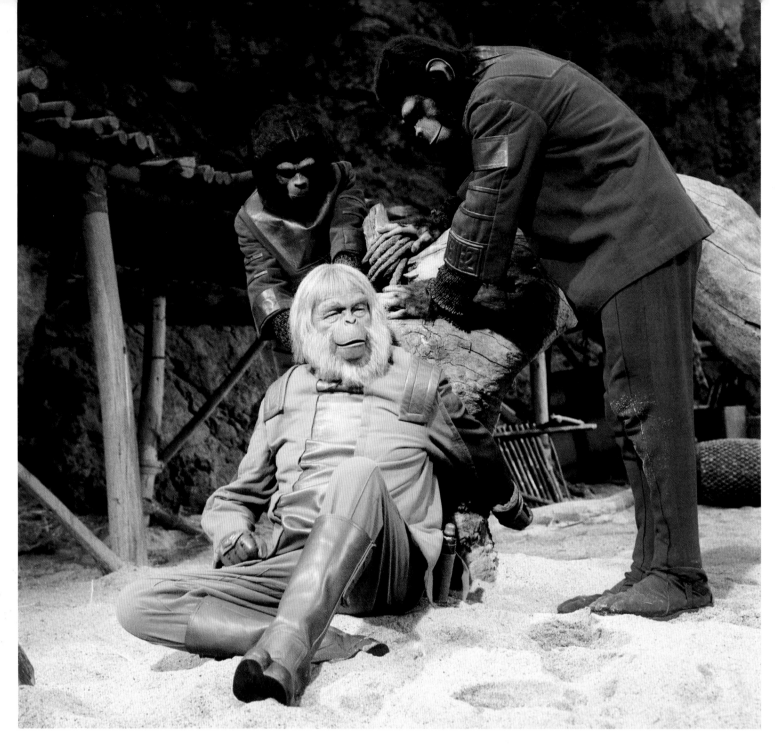

babies with a modern ape mother who is owned by a compassionate animal trainer (Ricardo Montalban) who plans to raise the baby. The film questioned how far governmental authority could extend over citizens—or even illegal aliens—and offered an ingenious theory of how humans lost control of the planet to simians.

In *Conquest of the Planet of the Apes* (1972), Cornelius and Zira's baby grows up to be Caesar (Roddy McDowall, who appeared in every ape film except *Beneath*). It's set in a dystopian American future where cats and dogs have been wiped out by a plague. Humans have taken apes as pets and then later use them as slaves (this history of how the apes evolved was related by Cornelius to the authorities in *Escape*). With Caesar in the lead, the slave apes stage an uprising and begin to take control, setting up what happens to Earth in the

future. The original five-movie saga resolves itself in *Battle for the Planet of the Apes* (1973). In it, Caesar fights against human and ape foes to establish a future in which humans and apes can co-exist peacefully.

The Apes movies are notable for much more than their makeup wizardry. Thematically, the five movies cover everything from race and class issues to religious fundamentalism, the Cold War, and mankind's inability to live in peace with one another. Beneath their "popcorn" veneer, these movies do what all great science fiction does—they make the viewer think.

Apes proved to be a very enduring and popular franchise, spawning both a live-action and animated television series in the 1970s and tons of merchandising, novelizations, and other product extensions. In 2001, a long-awaited remake of *Planet of the Apes* was finally released. Directed by

**Above**: *Kim Hunter (left), Maurice Evans, and Roddy McDowell spent weeks under John Chamber's revolutionary ape makeups in* Planet of the Apes.

**Top**: One of the massive sets of ruined New York (aided by a glass painting) from 1970's Beneath the Planet of the Apes. In the center are Linda Harrison and James Franciscus.

**Above**: This image from Planet of the Apes is now iconic, but in 1968 the revelation of the "alien" planet's identity was a shocker.

THE
FINAL
CHAPTER

in the incredible Apes saga.
The most suspenseful
showdown ever filmed
as two civilizations battle
for the right to inherit
what's left of the earth!

RODDY McDOWALL
as Caesar,
Supreme Ape Leader.

CLAUDE AKINS
as Aldo, Rebellious
Gorilla General.

NATALIE TRUNDY
as Lisa, Loving
Wife of Caesar.

SEVERN DARDEN
as Kolp, Radiation-
Crazed Mutant Leader.

LEW AYRES
as Mandemus,
The Peacemaker.

PAUL WILLIAMS
as Virgil, Orangutan
War Councilor.

JOHN HUSTON
as The Lawgiver.

# BATTLE FOR THE
# PLANET OF THE APES

20th CENTURY-FOX PRESENTS AN ARTHUR P. JACOBS PRODUCTION
"BATTLE FOR THE PLANET OF THE APES"
STARRING  RODDY McDOWALL · CLAUDE AKINS · NATALIE TRUNDY · SEVERN DARDEN · LEW AYRES · PAUL WILLIAMS · And JOHN HUSTON as The Lawgiver
DIRECTED BY J. LEE THOMPSON · PRODUCED BY ARTHUR P. JACOBS · ASSOCIATE PRODUCER FRANK CAPRA, JR. · SCREENPLAY BY JOHN WILLIAM CORRINGTON &
JOYCE HOOPER CORRINGTON · STORY BY PAUL DEHN · BASED UPON CHARACTERS CREATED BY PIERRE BOULLE · MUSIC BY LEONARD ROSENMAN
PANAVISION® · COLOR BY DE LUXE®

G  GENERAL AUDIENCES
All Ages Admitted

PANAVISION® · COLOR BY DE LUXE®

COPYRIGHT  1973 TWENTIETH CENTURY-FOX FILM CORPORATION

MP3009  63/132

*Above*: 1973's Battle for the Planet of the Apes,
the last film in the original series, cleverly set up
the means by which the apes take over Earth.

*Opposite top*: Actor Andy Serkis was transformed into the chimp Caesar through digital
animation in Rise of the Planet of the Apes.

*Opposite bottom*: Tim Roth, wearing Rick Baker's
redesigned ape makeup, in Tim Burton's 2001
remake of Planet of the Apes.

characters were created at least in part by computers. While it owes more to classic prison breakout films than the earlier *Apes* films, *Rise* echoes parts of *Conquest*. Caesar the chimp is again the protagonist, only now he has gained his human intelligence through being injected with a serum developed in hopes of curing Alzheimer's disease. When Caesar is forced to go to a shelter—actually a prison—for apes, he contrives to expose the others to an advanced version of the serum and then organizes them into a force. When the serum proves to be fatal to humans, the rest, as they say, is the future.

New Zealand's Weta Digital, the effects shop established by director Peter Jackson, created the apes in *Rise* through digital animation, as they had done for Jackson's 2005 remake of *King Kong*. Actor Andy Serkis, who had previously played Kong and Gollum in the *Lord of the Rings* trilogy, led a team of ape enactors whose performances were enhanced with, in Serkis's words, "digital makeup." For once, Serkis was not confined to a performance-capture stage during post-production. He could perform on set, even on location, wearing a special head-mounted camera that recorded every facial nuance for the animators. "The big leap forward for *Apes* was shooting every single scene with the other actors," he says.

As plans for a sequel to *Rise* are already in the works, it appears that the apes will continue to leap forward for some time to come.

Tim Burton, this version featured redesigned ape makeup from Oscar-winning makeup wizard Rick Baker and cameo appearances by original *Apes* movie actors Linda Harrison and Charlton Heston. That movie received mixed reviews from critics but did well at the box office.

More recently, the Apes franchise was rebooted again in 2011's *Rise of the Planet of the Apes*. In this version, the simian

# WHAT HAVE WE WROUGHT?

The postwar era not only brought new longings on the part of people to find their place in the universe, it also brought new and very real worries. The bombs that were dropped on Japan, ending World War II, were demonstrations of what science could do. What was not yet understood (and still may not be today) were the complete ramifications of exposure to radiation. Filmmakers increasingly turned their attentions to questions like that as the 1950s progressed. There was a new god in town during this time, and it was called the atomic bomb. It was no longer justification enough for a doctor or scientist to simply be "mad" in the manner of Dr. Cyclops, or hide behind the rationale of being a misunderstood, persecuted genius. Often in the films of this era, the characters thought they were acting out of righteous purpose, with sound, scientific backing to support them, but just as often, they were quite wrong.

**Above**: *Ray Harryhausen's title creature from 1953's* The Beast from 20,000 Fathoms *was an inspiration for Gojira (Godzilla) a year later.*

**Opposite**: *Destruction with a smile! Godzilla, King of the Monsters.*

### Gojira
#### *"Until I die, how can I be sure I won't be forced by someone to make the device again?"*

The first dramatization of the dangers that might be unleashed by atomic testing was depicted in 1953's *The Beast from 20,000 Fathoms*. It was based on the Ray Bradbury story "The Fog Horn" and featured special effects by Ray Harryhausen. In this film, the gigantic, metaphoric Pandora's box was the "Rhedosaurus," a prehistoric creature that was not mutated by radiation but simply thawed out after a nuclear test in the Arctic melted the thick ice inside which it had been trapped. Among those who appreciated the film was Japanese producer Tomoyuki Tanaka, who was planning a movie about an enormous, irradiated octopus. Once Tanaka saw Harryhausen's dinosaur-like creature and realized that his budget could not sustain the cost of stop-motion-animating a complex, tentacled creature, Tanaka's monster concept was revised to a dinosaur-like creature, to be played by a man in a suit.

In 1954's *Gojira* (the combination of "gorilla" and the Japanese word for beast, *kujira*), the existence of a gigantic, radiation-mutated creature that rises from the sea and wreaks havoc with its size and radioactive breath is first detected when a radiation-burned fishing boat is discovered. (The basic premise was based on a real incident in which a boat containing twenty-three fishermen was irradiated from a hydrogen bomb test in the Bikini atoll in 1954.) Gojira then shows up in person and destroys Japanese cities, causing a panic, until it can be vanquished employing yet another dangerous scientific discovery, a device that pulls all the oxygen from water. Essentially, Gojira is suffocated under the surface when the device is used.

Directed by Inoshiro Honda, *Gojira* was a serious-minded, noirish thriller with metaphoric overtones—the destruction of the cities (built in miniature by Eiji Tsurburaya) represented the destruction rendered by the bombs dropped on Hiroshima and Nagasaki. The decision over whether or not to use such weapons was further dramatized in the subplot involving the scientist who created the oxygen-removal device. As for the creature itself,

*Opposite top: The original big foot sighting from the 1998 remake of Godzilla.*

*Opposite bottom: This publicity shot for 1964's Godzilla vs. the Thing used a stock pose of Godzilla and matted into the other photo elements, with only middling success.*

**Above**: *The poster for the American version of Gojira, Godzilla, King of the Monsters.*

**Above right**: *Gojira/Godzilla is about to find out that water creatures and electricity don't mix.*

the decision to put actor Haru Nakajimi in a cumbersome dinosaur suit (which was so stifling he could stay inside for only three minutes at a time) resulted in a character that would become an icon of world cinema.

Gojira was a hit in Japan, and an even bigger hit in America in 1956 under its new title, *Godzilla, King of the Monsters*. For the U.S. version director Terry Morse cut the original footage—softening the anti-nuclear message and cutting out a subplot involving arranged marriage—dubbed what was left into English, and then filmed new scenes with Raymond Burr as a reporter named Steve Martin. The result was a more straightforward monster movie than a cautionary thriller. More than thirty Japanese-made, increasingly juvenile sequels followed, with Godzilla often the hero of the movie, protecting Japan from an array of other monsters—Mothra, Ghidora, and even King Kong in one film. The most notorious antagonist was the guest menace of 1971's *Godzilla vs. the Smog Monster*, which became the basis for a bizarre NBC comedy special that aired in 1977, hosted by John Belushi in a seedy Godzilla suit.

A big-budget American remake, simply titled *Godzilla*, released in 1998, and for the first time, Godzilla was created through digital animation. This Godzilla was sleeker, faster, and scarier, but it leveled New York City as effectively as it ever had Tokyo—and laid eggs to boot. Matthew Broderick starred, not as "Steve Martin," for obvious reasons, but as Nico Tatopoulos, a scientist studying the effects of radiation. His character was named after the artist who designed the digital Godzilla, Patrick Tatopoulos, whose sci-fi credits are long and distinguished. More recently, Tatopoulos recently became a judge on Syfy's popular series *Face Off*, a sci-fi makeup effects competition show.

**Above**: *Soldiers discover the giant ant in* Them!

**Left**: *The climactic shoot-out in the tunnel under Los Angeles in* Them!

*Left*: Joan Weldon has her picnic spoiled in a big way in 1954's Them!

*Below*: James Whitmore is about to feel the pinch in Them! *The special-effects ants in the movie itself are more effective than the publicity photos indicate.*

### Them!

#### "The atomic genie has been let out of the bottle."

In *Them!* (1954) the "them" in question are common ants that have been irradiated to monumental proportions because of nuclear testing in the New Mexico desert. The title comes from the screams of a small girl who bears witness to one of the ant attacks and, in shock, can only cry, "Them! Them! Them!" The authorities, including FBI agent Robert Graham (James Arness, who, along with his real-life brother, Peter Graves, were among the most familiar faces in 1950s sci-fi), have no clue as to what is out there, only that people in and around the desert are turning up dead in horrible and mysterious ways.

But government entomologist Dr. Harold Medford (Edmund Gwenn) and his scientist daughter Pat (Joan Weldon) recognize a giant footprint left at one of the scenes as that of an ant. What's more, a distinctive, eerie cry made by the twenty-foot monsters is detected. The U.S. Air Force gets involved, destroying one nest of eggs—but two flying queen ants stay on the loose and end up in the drainage spillways under Los Angeles for their final battle.

The first of the "big bug" subgenre that proliferated in the 1950s, *Them!* was originally envisioned as a Technicolor, 3-D spectacle. In the script, the climatic battle was to take place on the Santa Monica Pier, feature arcades and carnival rides, and show extensive special effects. However, right before filming began the studio slashed the budget, forcing director Gordon Douglas to drop the plans for 3-D and the costly special effects and shoot the picture in black and white. What was left were the giant ants, large-scale practical props manipulated by a team of crewmen. But there was only enough money left in the downsized budget to construct two of them; one complete model and one with only the head and thorax, though a few background ants with limited mobility were also constructed. *Them!* also contained another early sighting of actor Leonard Nimoy, who turns up in a bit part as a soldier.

**Above**: James Mason, Paul Lukas, and Ted de Corsia paddle out to the Nautilus in 20,000 Leagues Under the Sea.

**Opposite top**: James Mason as Captain Nemo and Paul Lukas as Professor Arronax take in the underwater sights in 20,000 Leagues Under the Sea..

**Opposite bottom**: The futuristic/Victorian design of 20,000 Leagues Under the Sea was a seminal influence on the movement now known as Steampunk.

Despite the last-minute compromises, *Them!* was very well received and garnered good reviews. It seemed that the only person who didn't like the film was studio head Jack L. Warner, who reportedly told his staff that anyone who wanted to make another ant movie would be sent to Republic Studios, which was considered the Siberia of the studio system. He may have changed his opinion, though, when *Them!* became Warner Bros.' highest grossing film of that year.

### 20,000 Leagues Under the Sea
*"I have done with society for reasons that seem good to me. Therefore, I do not obey its laws."*

Jules Verne's *20,000 Leagues Under the Sea* was one of the first novels ever adapted to film, appearing as early as 1907—only two years after Verne's death—in an adaptation directed by Georges Méliès. Universal Pictures produced its own version of the story in 1916, which featured some of the earliest underwater photography ever screened. But it is the 1954 Walt Disney version that features the classic depiction of Verne's antisocial genius Captain Nemo.

Nemo (James Mason) is the builder and captain of the *Nautilus*, a massive, fish-shaped submarine that has the ability to sustain itself and its crew under water almost indefinitely. Disillusioned with society aboveground, particularly those nations that have become empires, Nemo sets out to destroy their warships in the name of saving those souls the weapons would have killed during conflict. The world at large, however, knows nothing of Nemo or his craft, so the destruction he wreaks is thought to be the work of a sea monster. Professor Arronax (Paul Lukas), his manservant Conseil (Peter Lorre), and a whaler named Ned Land (Kirk Douglas) are all aboard a ship sent to investigate, and the ship is subsequently scuttled. The trio is taken aboard the *Nautilus*, and there they learn the truth about the mysterious Captain Nemo.

While Disney had already produced a handful of live-action adventure films in England, chiefly to utilize box office returns that were frozen there, *20,000 Leagues under the Sea* was his first made-in-the-U.S.A. live-action film (though animation was employed to create the fish seen through the windows of the *Nautilus*). Disney spared no expense, building a large-scale model mock-up for the *Nautilus* with lavish interiors, complete with ceilings, and sending the cast and crew to the Bahamas for underwater filming.

The film's major action set piece, a battle between the *Nautilus* and a giant squid, proved problematic. Rather than animate the creature in miniature, Disney ordered a gigantic mechanical squid with forty-foot-long tentacles be built and that the scene be filmed in the studio tank. When the rushes revealed that it looked like a huge marionette on strings and that even the cast seemed to be laughing at it, Disney ordered director Richard Fleischer to move on to other scenes and appointed second-unit director James C. Havens take over the squid battle. Havens and production designer Harper Goff developed the idea of staging the scene during a violent storm, which not only heightened the drama but also masked the wires. They got Disney to sign off on the approach, which cost an extra $200,000. By the time shooting wrapped, *20,000 Leagues* had become the most expensive Hollywood film to date, costing about $5 million.

Disney used his then-new ABC television show *Disneyland* to promote *20,000 Leagues Under the Sea*, which became a huge hit and won Oscars for special effects and art direction. The film can claim two other legacies: the first is that it launched a brief Jules Verne craze, which included the films *From the Earth to the Moon* (1958); *Journey to the Center of the Earth* (1959); *The Mysterious Island* (1961), the sequel to *20,000 Leagues,* which featured special effects by Ray Harryhausen; *Master of the World* (1961), something of a redo of *20,000 Leagues*, only with a flying craft instead of an underwater craft and a misguided genius named Robur instead of Nemo; and *Five Weeks in a Balloon* (1962). Its long-term legacy is its lavish sets and props, which were inspired by how a Victorian might see the future, and virtually created the blueprint for what is now known as steampunk.

Interestingly, director Richard Fleisher was the son of animation producer Max Fleischer, Disney's chief rival in the 1920s and '30s.

**Above left**: *A Ray Harryhausen model of a giant underwater creature attack from 1961's* The Mysterious Island.

**Above right**: *Vincent Price played another of Jules Verne's mad geniuses, Captain Robur, in 1961's* Master of the World.

**Opposite top**: *The giant squid attack from* 20,000 Leagues Under the Sea *(1954) was completely re-filmed against a studio-made tempest.*

**Opposite bottom**: *Kirk Douglas battling a tentacle in* 20,000 Leagues Under the Sea.

GIANT SPIDER STRIKES!
..CRAWLING TERROR 100 FEET HIGH!

Universal-International presents

TARANTULA!

STARRING

JOHN AGAR
MARA CORDAY
LEO G. CARROLL

with NESTOR PAIVA · ROSS ELLIOTT

DIRECTED BY JACK ARNOLD · SCREENPLAY BY ROBERT M. FRESCO AND MARTIN BERKELEY · PRODUCED BY WILLIAM ALLAND

Courtesy of Universal Pictures.

*Left*: Tarantula *was one of the better Universal sci-fi/horror hybrids of the 1950s.*

*Opposite top*: This puppet tarantula was used for close-ups and stunt sequences in Tarantula; for other shots, a real arachnid starred.

*Opposite bottom left*: Mara Corday is snug on a rug, fighting a bug in Tarantula.

*Opposite bottom right*: Leo G. Carroll played the scientist who created the monster arachnid in the lab in Tarantula, and lived to regret it.

**Tarantula**
**"The isotope triggered our nutrient into a nightmare."**

The star of 1955's *Tarantula* is evident from the title. In his quest to solve the world's hunger problem, Professor Gerald Deemer (Leo G. Carroll) develops an atomic-enhanced growth nutrient that he intends to use to feed animals. Feed them it does; it also makes them grow to monstrous proportions, particularly a desert tarantula, which becomes enlarged to the size of a train car and takes off into the Arizona desert, dining on cattle and menacing humans.

*Tarantula*'s producer William Alland had been an actor in Orson Welles's infamous radio adaptation of *The War of the Worlds*, and also played the reporter trailing "Rosebud" in Welles's *Citizen Kane*. By the 1950s he had abandoned acting and, along with director Jack Arnold, was responsible for most of Universal Pictures' sci-fi/monster movies of the era. *Tarantula* was unique in that, except for a few close-up shots of a hairy mechanical spider, the irradiated menace was played by an actual arachnid. Special effects cinematographer Clifford Stine filmed a real tarantula on miniature sets, directing its movements by shooting little spurts of air at it. These shots were combined optically with scenes involving the actors, providing a level of reality that even stop-motion animation could not achieve. For the fiery finale, jet pilot Clint Eastwood (yes, Clint Eastwood, in his fourth movie) shoots a napalm rocket at the tarantula and ignites it. For this last sequence a model spider was used; it was created by Wah Chang, who would soon become a major figure in the art of special effects in both film and television.

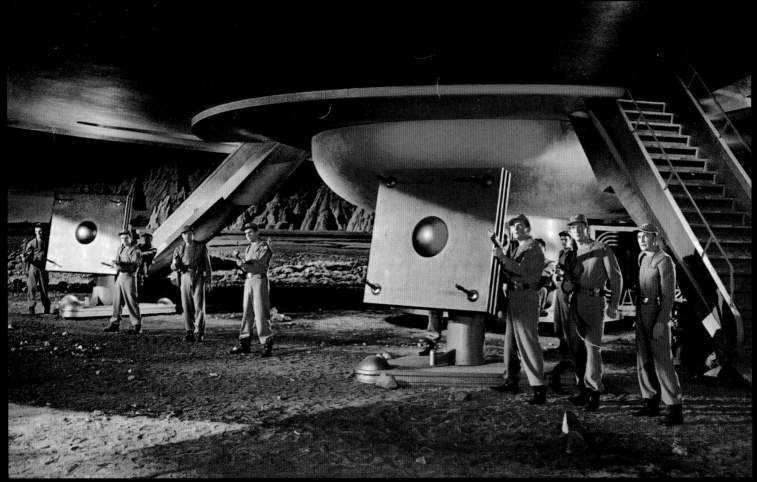

## Forbidden Planet

### "My evil self is at the door!"

No less than William Shakespeare provided the inspiration for *Forbidden Planet* (1956), a lavish vision of the twenty-third century loosely based on Shakespeare's *The Tempest* (also the source of the phrase "brave new world" that would develop a sci-fi pedigree of its own). Instead of the vengeful magician Prospero stranded on an island with his daughter and a sprite assistant, the film depicts Professor Morbius (Walter Pidgeon) stranded on the far-off planet Altair IV, with his daughter Alta (Anne Francis) and a robot assistant named Robby. Morbius is not a magician; but he has expanded his intelligence beyond normal human level by communing with the energy of the planet's previous inhabitants, the Krell, which is stored in a vast underground machine.

A rocket ship crew captained by Commander John Adams (Leslie Nielsen) is sent to find out what happened to a previous expedition to Altair IV. They discover Morbius alive but unwilling to allow them to land on the planet, because he does not wish to share his newfound knowledge with the people of Earth. They land anyway, and in time discover that a lethal, invisible monster haunts the planet, a monster that turns out to be the melding of the Krell energy with Morbius's own prejudices. Once Morbius realizes that *he* is the deadly monster, he fights it, sustaining mortal injuries, and decides to blow up the planet. Alta, Robby the Robot, and the crew escape.

Produced by MGM, a studio not generally known for its science fiction, *Forbidden Planet* featured spectacular special effects for its time, supervised by veteran effects artist A. Arnold Gillespie. The Great Machine of the Krells, which appears on screen to be an endless pit filled with computer technology, and the spaceship that brings Adams's crew to the planet were elaborate models. A total of three model ships were constructed, the smallest of which was twenty inches in diameter while the largest was six feet in diameter. There was also a full-scale mock-up that filled most of a soundstage. When the so-called monster of the Id, the physical manifestation of Morbius's mind combined with the Krell intelligence, was finally seen, it was actually an animated cartoon created by Disney artist Joshua Meador, who also animated laser blasts for the film. Cinematographer George Folsey

*Above: Robby the Robot gets the drop on astronauts Jack Kelly, Warren Stevens, and Leslie Nielsen, at the behest of Walter Pidgeon, in Forbidden Planet.*

*Opposite top: Commander Adams (Leslie Nielsen, in his pre-comedy days) confronts Professor Mobius (Walter Pidgeon) and Alta (Anne Francis) in Forbidden Planet.*

*Opposite bottom: Forbidden Planet was a major big-budget extravaganza, with lavish sets and effects and lush color.*

admitted at the time that lighting the futuristic look of the sets made of metal, glass, and plastic without showing a telltale lamp glare on camera was often a nightmare. The film's unusual, eerie score was created by Bebe and Louis Barron, who used no instruments of any kind—not even a theramin—but created sounds by putting electronic circuits through an amplifier in what is perhaps the first purely electronic music.

*Forbidden Planet* established a theme that would recur often in sci-fi, that of a crew sent out in space to discover what happened to a previous mission only to find far more than it anticipated. What the film is best remembered for, however, is the appearance of Robby the Robot. Designed by Bob Kinoshita, Robby was the first screen robot with a genuine personality, and while studio publicity of the time put forth that Robby moved as a result of six electric motors controlled through a switchboard panel, it was really 1940s actor-turned-stuntman Frankie Darro inside the suit. Robby the Robot would go on to have a career of his own, appearing in a subsequent MGM film, *The Invisible Boy* (1957), and a host of television shows, including *The Addams Family*, *The Monkees*, *Columbo*, *Mork and Mindy*, *Lost in Space*, and even *The Love Boat*.

### Invasion of the Body Snatchers
#### *"They're here already! You're next!"*
In the science fiction subgenre of paranoiac hysteria, the all-time champion remains 1956's *Invasion of the Body Snatchers*. Directed by Don Siegel and script by film noir specialist Daniel Mainwaring, which in turn was based on a novel by Jack Finney, the picture is considered by many to be another Cold War–era allegory about alien (read *Communist*) infiltration of society. Some critics feel that the movie is actually a statement about McCarthyism, while still others believe that the movie is really about the loss of individualism in our increasingly mechanized and impersonal society. All that said, these themes are fairly deeply buried beneath a frightening tale of organisms born out of gigantic seed pods that take over the people in the small town of Santa Mira, California.

Dr. Miles Bennell (Kevin McCarthy) initially doesn't believe his patients who claim that their close relatives are somehow different, but he slowly learns that an alien force is taking over the citizenry. The process happens during sleep, so Miles forces himself and his lady friend Becky Driscoll (Dana Wynter) to stay awake. Unfortunately, Becky succumbs to sleep. In a now-iconic scene, a disheveled, raving Bennell tries to stop traffic in an attempt to warn people—including the audience—that they could be next in the insidious takeover plot.

Siegel and Mainwaring wanted to end the movie this way. But Allied Artists, the studio behind the film, forced them to include a bookend prologue and epilogue in which Bennell, having been picked up and taken to the hospital, relates his wild story in flashback, only to be exonerated at the end when seedpods are discovered by others.

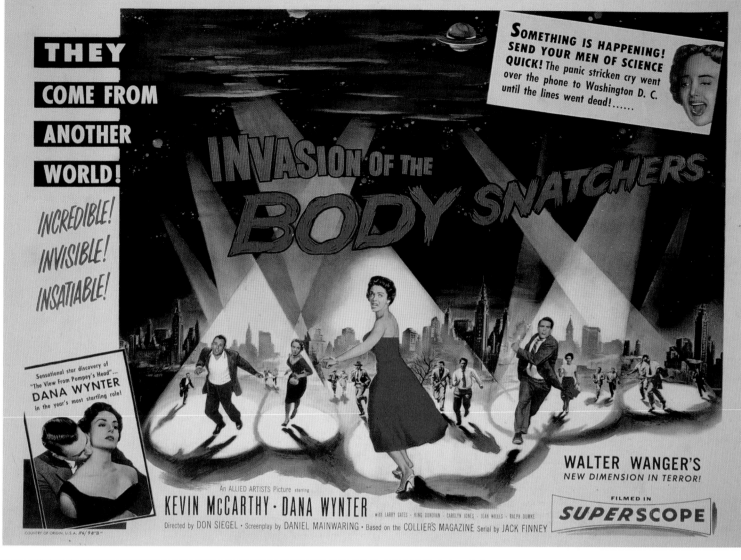

THEY COME FROM ANOTHER WORLD!

INCREDIBLE! INVISIBLE! INSATIABLE!

SOMETHING IS HAPPENING! SEND YOUR MEN OF SCIENCE QUICK! The panic stricken cry went over the phone to Washington D. C. until the lines went dead!......

INVASION OF THE BODY SNATCHERS

Sensational star discovery of "The View from Pompey's Head"... DANA WYNTER in the year's most startling role!

An ALLIED ARTISTS Picture starring
KEVIN McCARTHY · DANA WYNTER
with LARRY GATES · KING DONOVAN · CAROLYN JONES · JEAN WILLES · RALPH DUMKE
Directed by DON SIEGEL · Screenplay by DANIEL MAINWARING · Based on the COLLIER'S MAGAZINE Serial by JACK FINNEY

COUNTRY OF ORIGIN, U.S.A. 56/98°B

WALTER WANGER'S NEW DIMENSION IN TERROR!

FILMED IN SUPERSCOPE

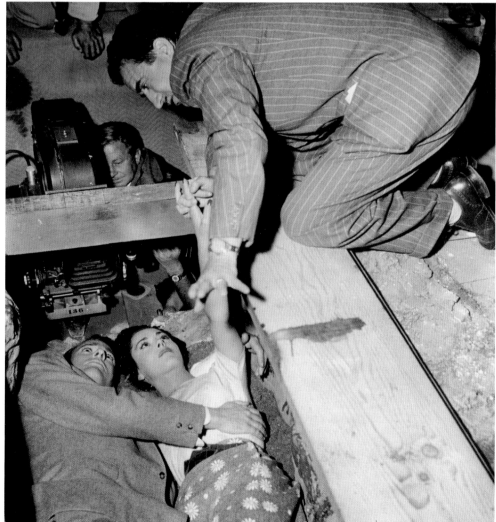

**Above**: *The original* Invasion of the Body Snatchers *has been taken both as a metaphor for Communist encroachment, or a warning against blind paranoia about it.*

**Left**: *Director Don Siegel rehearses actors Kevin McCarthy and Dana Wynter, whose characters are attempting to hide from the transformed mob in* Invasion of the Body Snatchers.

**Opposite top**: *If the "Id Monster" from* Forbidden Planet *looks like an evil toon, that's because it is; it was animated by Disney artist Joshua Meador.*

**Opposite bottom**: *Robby the Robot from* Forbidden Planet *went on to a long career in Hollywood.*

**Top**: In the classic original ending of 1956's Invasion of the Body Snatchers, *Kevin McCarthy* screams, "They're here already! You're next! You're next!"

**Above**: Kevin McCarthy destroys a pod from which the overtaken earthlings emerge in Invasion of the Body Snatchers.

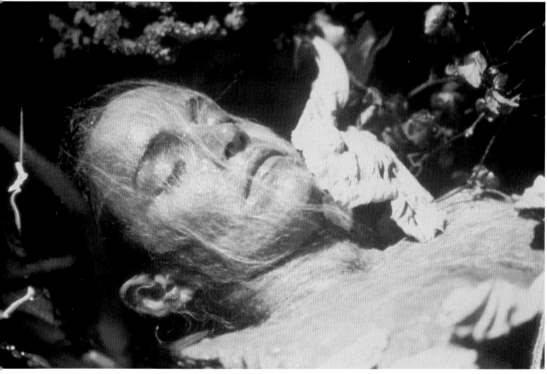

A remake of *Invasion of the Body Snatchers*, starring Donald Sutherland, Brooke Adams, and Leonard Nimoy, came out in 1978, and the twenty-two-year gap between the two films was quite discernable. Full nudity could be now shown on screen (the pod people are, after all, born without clothing, something the original could only imply), and far more graphic special effects were available, notably for a scene in which a pod version of Donald Sutherland is killed by chopping its face in half with a garden hoe. Instead of the small-town setting of the original, the 1978 version was set in San Francisco; Kevin McCarthy returned for a cameo, reprising his traffic-stopping rant. The original film's director Don Siegel also showed up as a cab driver. Finney's novel was adapted in 1993 for the somewhat less successful *Body Snatchers*, and again in 2007, when Nicole Kidman and Daniel Craig starred in a semi-remake entitled *The Invasion*, which was structured more as a paranoia thriller than an overt sci-fi film.

*Top*: Nicole Kidman in The Invasion (2007), the most recent remake of Invasion of the Body Snatchers.

*Above left*: Brooke Adams in mid-transformation in 1978's Invasion of the Body Snatchers.

*Above right*: Donald Sutherland and Brooke Adams try to outrun the pod people in the 1978 remake of Invasion of the Body Snatchers, which moves the action from a small town to San Francisco.

Once it was human... even as you and I!

# SHE HAD TO KILL THE THING HER HUSBAND HAD BECOME—

**BUT COULD SHE?**

# The Fly

**IN CINEMASCOPE AND TERROR-COLOR BY DE LUXE**

FOR YOUR OWN GOOD WE URGE YOU NOT TO SEE IT ALONE!

THE MONSTER CREATED BY ATOMS GONE WILD!

AL HEDISON · PATRICIA OWENS · VINCENT PRICE · HERBERT MARSHALL · KURT NEUMANN · JAMES CLAVELL · Based on a Story by GEORGE LANGELAAN

*Above: The hyped-up poster for* The Fly *(1958) played down the film's scientific angle and gave the impression it was another "big-bug" radiation movie.*

*Opposite top: A special camera lens created the "fly's-eye-view" shot of Patricia Owens in* The Fly.

*Opposite bottom: Patricia Owens puts her husband (David Hedison) out of his misery in* The Fly.

## The Fly
### "Helllp me—helllllllllp meee!"

These days, the original *The Fly* (1958), starring Vincent Price and David Hedison (billed as Al Hedison), is largely relegated to the status of a campy, scary, little B movie. It was not regarded that way at the time of its release: it was initially hailed as a "weird masterpiece," and its $700,000 budget was noted in the press as being surprisingly substantial for this sort of film. Its studio, 20th Century Fox, was so confident in the actual scientific basis for the film that it allowed technical consultant Dr. Frank Creswell to state in public that an atomic transference machine as is depicted in the film—which can break organisms down to atoms, shoot the atoms across distances, and then reassemble them—would actually become a reality within the decade. Instead, we landed on the moon. But this does show how the perspective of a film can be altered by the passage of time.

Written by James Clavell, who would later achieve fame for such epic-length novels as *Shogun* and *Tai-Pan*, adapted from a short story by George Langelaan, and directed by Kurt Neumann (*Rocketship X-M*), *The Fly* is presented in flashback form. It begins with the seeming murder of scientist André Delambre (Hedison) by his wife Helene (Patricia Owens), by way of a massive press that squishes his head and arm into pulp. However, through the course of the flashback, André's brother François (Price) learns that André invented an atomic transporter through which he transported himself in the unwelcome presence of a housefly. André ended up with the fly's head and arm, while the fly ended up with André's head and arm! André's death is really suicide, though the police, represented by Inspector Charas (Herbert Marshall), refuse to believe it. The eventual discovery of the fly that was inside the transport chamber with Delambre—which now has his tiny head and arm—exonerates Helen.

During filming, Hedison suffered bruises and cuts to his face in a car accident, which for any other film shoot would have caused expensive delays or rescheduling, but for *The Fly*, it didn't matter. By that point in the filming Hedison's face was hidden under a hideous fly mask crafted by makeup artist Ben Nye out of plastic, paint, and turkey feathers. Because the fly eyes were opaque, the actor had difficulty seeing. He also had difficulty breathing. The plastic eye shells were moved slightly to allow for an opening, solving both problems. Michael Rennie (*The Day the Earth Stood Still*) was originally sought for the role

*Above*: Charles Herbert and Vincent Price spot the fly that ended up with the human head and hand, from The Fly.

*Left*: David Hedison as The Fly.

**Left**: Jeff Goldblum is unrecogniz-
able in mid-fly transformation in
David Cronenberg's 1986 remake of
The Fly.

**Below**: The "brundlething" from
1986's The Fly.

of André, and while he might have been more convincing physically
as Vincent Price's brother, Rennie did not want to spend half of his
screen time made up as a common house pest.

The film's most famous scene is the climax, in which the fly
with Hedison's head is found trapped in a spider web and screams
for help. The close-up shows a terrified Hedison trapped in a web
made of rubber cement, but for the reaction shot of Price and
Marshall, a tiny mechanical fly was placed in a web, while an off-
camera voice screamed, "Help me!" The scene proved to be too
much for the veteran actors, who could not keep a straight face.
"Help *you*?" Marshall finally cried out of frustration, after the ump-
teenth ruined take, "To hell with you! Help *us*!" Still, *The Fly* became
a huge hit, though director Neumann would never know that, having
died shortly after the film premiered.

Canadian director David Cronenberg directed a large-scale, criti-
cally acclaimed remake of *The Fly* in 1986, starring Jeff Goldblum as
unfortunate scientist Seth Brundle. Unlike the first film, in which the
fly and human parts were neatly redistributed, this version featured
icky, dripping makeup effects, created by Chris Walas, in seven
stages, from human to . . . well, to something dubbed the "brundlething." Walas's gruesome effects won the film an Oscar for Best
Makeup. Cronenberg's film would inspire an opera version of *The Fly*,
with music and libretto by Howard Shore and David Henry Hwang.

### The Outer Limits
### *"We control the vertical; we control the horizontal."*

Before each episode of *The Outer Limits*—an hour-long sci-fi
television series that premiered on ABC in 1963—actually began,
viewers were told that they had surrendered control of their sets,
as befitting the show's original title, *Please Stand By*. "We are
controlling transmission," said the unidentified voice (actor Vic
Perrin). "For the next hour, sit quietly and we will control all you
see and hear." Who, exactly, "we" were was never explained, though
the slightly ominous opening effectively tapped into the general
unease of the time that somebody, somewhere—either Big Brother
on Earth, or something with multiple eyes from another planet—
might be watching our every move. If nothing else, it delivered the
fact that *The Outer Limits*, which was created by writer/producer
Leslie Stevens, was not messing around.

THE SCIENCE FICTION UNIVERSE . . . AND BEYOND

*Above: Most episodes of* The Outer Limits *featured strange creatures up close and personal.*

*The Outer Limits* was a mix of in-your-face sci-fi and horror. Most episodes featured a creature of some sort, dubbed "the bear" by the show's production staff, and series producer Joseph Stefano's stated goal was to frighten viewers. Frequently the bears were aliens, such as the creature from "The Galaxy Being," which was made to look even eerier by showing it on screen in negative, and the Zantis from "The Zanti Misfits," which looked like tarantulas with satyr faces. But they could also be earthlings time-warped through thousands of years of evolutionary history, as in "The Sixth Finger," which featured elaborate prosthetic makeup by John Chambers, who in the next few years would design Mr. Spock's pointed ears for *Star Trek* and develop the simian makeup for *Planet of the Apes*. Special effects artists Wah Chang, Tim Barr, Ralph Rodine, and model animator Jim Danforth created many of the effects for the program. The show always ended with the Voice telling viewers that they had been returned to normal life . . . until next week.

While popular with audiences, critics were less kind to *The Outer Limits*. For its second season, the bears were for the most part caged, while more of the stories favored the tone of "Controlled Experiment," a first-season episode that featured Barry Morse and Carroll O'Connor as a Martian Holmes-and-Watson act, who replay a shooting over and over from every angle and speed to try and understand the concept of murder. The show was canceled in January of 1965, but it was well remembered enough to revive in 1995. The new *The Outer Limits* actually ran longer than the original—a total of seven seasons, airing first on Showtime and later seasons on Syfy—and though Leslie Stevens and Joseph Stefano both returned as consultants, the emphasis shifted away from the weekly bears that had marked their original collaboration.

**Above**: Burgess Meredith in "Time Enough at Last," a favorite episode among fans of The Twilight Zone.

**Opposite**: The title card from the 1985 redo of The Twilight Zone.

myopic nuclear-blast survivor who finally has all the time in the world to read but then breaks his glasses. This episode also demonstrated the show's penchant for grim irony and twist endings. Other episodes, such as "Walking Distance" and "The Trouble with Templeton," focused on the wistful longing for the past in a rapidly changing world. A few episodes bordered on outright horror, such as the famous "Nightmare at 20,000 Feet," starring William Shatner as a mental patient on an airplane who sees a monster on the wing through the cabin window, and "The New Exhibit," an hour-long episode in which the wax figures of murderers seem to come to life. (The show extended to one hour long for its fourth season, but returned to its better-suited half-hour format for the fifth and final season.)

For all its influence, *The Twilight Zone* was never at the top of the ratings, and it went off the air in 1964. Serling moved on, eventually developing *Night Gallery*, a series devoted more to supernatural horror than sci-fi and sometimes tinged with a strange comedic tone,.

In 1982, seven years after Serling's death, producer Steven Spielberg decided it was time to return to the Zone, this time for the big screen. For *Twilight Zone: The Movie* he assembled an A-list directing team—*Mad Max* director George Miller, Joe Dante, John Landis, and himself. Spielberg opted to structure the film as a portmanteau, with four stories and a wraparound, choosing "Nightmare at 20,000 Feet," "It's a Good Life" (the original starred young Billy Mumy as a horrific little kid who terrorizes everyone through his ability to control reality), "Kick the Can" (in which seniors revert to children by playing), and a new segment, scripted and directed by Landis. That story, which centered on a familiar *Twilight Zone* theme of a bigot who is magically forced to walk in the shoes of those he hates, came closest to recapturing the spirit of the original show, though its running time was truncated due to an on-set accident with the segment's star, Vic Morrow. That tragedy, which also took the lives of two children, served to overshadow whatever *Twilight Zone: The Movie* might or might not have achieved.

The original 156 episodes of the series covered just about every style and sub-genre of sci-fi: space travel (as in "And When the Sky Opened Up," in which three astronauts mysteriously vanish after returning to Earth); artificial intelligence ("The Mighty Casey," about a robot ball player); time travel ("The Odyssey of Flight 33," in which an airline is caught in a time warp); post-apocalyptic ("The Old Man in the Cave," in which a reclusive, godlike being governs a bombed-out society); aliens ("The Invaders," starring Agnes Moorehead as a farm woman besieged by creatures from outer space); and alien paranoia ("The Monsters Are Due on Maple Street," in which a small town is pushed into destroying itself by alien suggestion).

Given the era—the show ran from 1959 to 1964—many stories dealt with the Cold War and the atomic bomb, such as "The Shelter" and "Time Enough at Last." The latter starred Burgess Meredith as a mousy,

**Above left**: Rod Serling.

**Above right**: Earl Holliman in the Twilight Zone pilot episode, "Where Is Everybody?"

**Right**: Vic Morrow in Twilight Zone: The Movie, the film in which he would lose his life in a tragic on-set accident.

**Opposite top**: John Lithgow fights a gremlin on an airplane wing in the remake of "Nightmare at 20,000 Feet," from 1983's Twilight Zone: The Movie.

**Opposite bottom**: William Shatner and Nick Cravat in "Nightmare at 20,000 Feet" on The Twilight Zone. Cravat's bathrobe and unfinished makeup indicate this photo was taken during rehearsal.

The Twilight Zone returned as a television series two years later, first as an hour-long anthology and then in half-hour format. Notable writers such as Harlan Ellison, Ray Bradbury, and Stephen King were represented, but overall the series seemed more fascinated by makeup and special effects than with the human heart and soul. Another new version of the show emerged in 2002 with the best intentions—it covered the kinds of social issues that Rod Serling loved to address—but it barely made a blip and was canceled after one season.

Shortly before he died at age fifty, Serling made a startling confession to an interviewer. "God knows, when I look back over thirty years of professional writing, I'm hard-pressed to come up with anything that's important," he said. "Some things are literate, some things are interesting, some things are classy, but very damn little is important." Granted, like beauty, importance is in the eye of the beholder. But if Serling had only possessed the kind of time machine he occasionally wrote about and that could have propelled him to the present day, he could see for himself just how firmly both he and The Twilight Zone have been etched into our collective consciousness.

Throughout the first half of the 1960s, a strange thing began to happen to science fiction on film and television: it seemed as though time was beginning to move forward and backward at the same time. Some films were set in the past, but featured such futuristic themes as space travel. Others were set in the near future but were inspired by classic eighteenth- and nineteenth-century literature, such as *Robinson Crusoe*. Still others boasted of futuristic settings, yet the visual style was straight from a 1940s crime drama—let's call this "noirpunk." Maybe it was a sign that, as the reality of science fact continued to press toward the stars, we still needed to be comforted by that which was familiar.

*Above*: Rod Taylor, director George Pal, and Yvette Mimieux on the set of The Time Machine (1960).

*Opposite top*: The Time Machine in "futuristic Metrocolor!" There was nothing futuristic about Metrocolor, the color system trademarked by MGM, but it sounded good.

*Opposite bottom*: The time machine from The Time Machine.

### The Time Machine
#### *"When I speak of time, I'm speaking of the fourth dimension."*

Producer George Pal tended to concentrate on sci-fi films that were semi-documentary in nature, such as *Destination Moon* and *When Worlds Collide* and 1955's *Conquest of Space*, which predicted a working space station and a journey to the surface of Mars. However, once Pal stepped into the director's chair his films became far more fanciful—even more fanciful than the marauding Martians in *The War of the Worlds*. *The Time Machine* (1960), based on another H. G. Wells novel, was Pal's second feature-film directorial effort; instead of utilizing scientifically based equipment, such as rocket ships, this time the protagonist zooms back and forth in time in a quaintly Victorian contraption that works simply because it works.

Having announced his incredible discovery to unbelieving friends, the time traveler, George (Rod Taylor), leaves the comfortable Victorian world of 1900 and travels beyond the two world wars and on to the ultimate nuclear conflict, which takes place in 1966. From there he blasts into the future, landing in the year 802,701, a time when civilization has been altered beyond recognition. There are two cultures in this far-future world: the Eloi, a light-skinned, ungoverned sun people who returned to the surface to live once the radioactive atmosphere was safe again; and the monstrous Morlocks, shaggy-haired, teal-skinned semi-simians, who evolved underground. The Morlocks brutalize and even cannibalize the Eloi. George falls in love with the beautiful Eloi Weena (Yvette Mimieux) and struggles against the Morlocks. While he manages to defeat the Morlocks, he is trapped in their underground lair. He escapes using his machine, returns briefly to 1900, and then he travels forward again to 802,701 in order to live out his days in a Morlock-free paradise with Weena.

Stop-motion animation was used to simulate the passage of time from George's point of view. The effects include the almost instant creation and destruction of buildings, the growth of plants, and even the gruesome decomposition of a dead Morlock. A special effects house called Projects Unlimited, which was established by Gene Warren, Tim Barr, and Wah Chang, handled the Oscar-winning effects. For scenes involving Taylor, the rapid passage of time was represented by spinning a wheel with many colors in front of a light, which simulated sunrise, high noon, sunset, and darkness within seconds. The signature prop of the film was the time machine itself, resembling a sled upon the back of which was attached a large, rotating wheel,

and which bore a plaque reading "Manufactured by H. George Wells," just in case audiences did not get the significance of the hero's name, George.

While publicizing the film, Pal enjoyed playing the role of visionary; he predicted that man would walk on the moon by 1966, and also, more prosaically, he predicted the invention of the microwave oven.

A big-screen remake of *The Time Machine* was released in 2002, directed by Simon Wells, a former animation director. Despite his lack of live-action background, Wells came by the project honestly by being the great-grandson of H. G. Wells. This version begins in 1899; the time traveler, Alexander (Guy Pearce), creates his time machine in order to go back and save his fiancée from being murdered—which he does—only to see her killed by accident. Going forward into the future, he lands in 2030 and 2037 before ending up in 802,701 in the time of the Eloi and the Morlocks. For this version, effects wizard Stan Winston created animatronic Morlock masks. There were up to thirty-two tiny servo motors in each mask for expression control, and a tiny camera lens positioned in each nose, which was the only means through which the actors inside could see.

While an entirely new time machine was built for this version (though like the original it contained a barber's chair), the original does still exist. In the early 1970s, it was auctioned off with hundreds of other props and costumes by MGM, but somehow its base ended up in a thrift shop in Orange, California. It was rescued from the shop and, with George Pal's assistance, restored by Hollywood sci-fi/horror collector Bob Burns, who has it today.

H. G. Wells's *Time Machine* story has actually formed the basis of many movie and television plots. In Syfy's 2011 made-for-television film *Morlocks*, a military experiment with time travel opens up a portal to the future into which Morlocks invade the present day. And in Syfy's *Warehouse 13* television series, H. G. Wells himself (or actually *herself* in the case of this show) becomes a major recurring character.

### First Men in the Moon

**"Soon others will be coming from Earth; our galleries will be strewn with dead."**

*First Men in the Moon* (1964), produced by Charles H. Schneer and directed by Nathan Juran, is the Ray Harryhausen film that is unfamiliar even to some Harryhausen fans. Schneer and Harryhausen had already made the classics *The 7th Voyage of Sinbad* (1958, also directed by Juran), *Mysterious Island* (1961), and *Jason and the Argonauts* (1963), all filmed in "Dynamation," the name Harryhausen gave to his painstaking animation technique. But *First Men in the Moon* was an unusual project for them in that it was driven less by Harryhausen's animation wizardry than it was by plot. It was also the only Dynamation film to be shot in widescreen format.

Told in the then-popular flashback format, the film begins with modern astronauts traveling to the moon in a United Nations–sponsored mission, only to find a Union Jack and

*Above: A "moon cow" from* The First Men in the Moon *(1964), animated by Ray Harryhausen.*

*Opposite top: The fearsome Morlocks from 1960's* The Time Machine.

*Opposite bottom: Guy Pearce piloted a more modernistic time travel device in the 2002 remake of* The Time Machine.

**H.G. WELLS' ASTOUNDING ADVENTURE IN**
**DYNAMATION !**

COLUMBIA PICTURES
presents a
CHARLES H.
SCHNEER
production

H.G. WELLS'
**FIRST MEN IN THE MOON**

IN PANAVISION · *LUNA*COLOR · DYNAMATION

starring
**EDWARD JUDD·MARTHA HYER** and **LIONEL JEFFRIES**
Screenplay by
NIGEL KNEALE and JAN READ
Associate Producer RAY HARRYHAUSEN · Directed by NATHAN JURAN · AN AMERAN FILM

*Above*: Panavision was real; Dynamation was real; but LUNACOLOR?

*Opposite top*: Lionel Jeffries and Edward Judd try to get used to the gravity on the moon in The First Men in the Moon.

*Opposite bottom*: Lionel Jeffries and Martha Hyer meet the Selenites, here played by children in locust-like suits.

a note claiming the moon for Queen Victoria! Tracing the names on the note, U.N. representatives find an elderly man named Arnold Bedford (Edward Judd) in an old folks' home, and he tells a strange story of a lunar landing that took place in 1899. With him on the mission were the eccentric, cold-prone Professor Cavor (Lionel Jeffries) and Bedford's fiancée, Kate Callender (Martha Hyer). They arrived there in a Victorian craft propelled by Cavorite, a gravity-defying substance invented by the professor. On the moon they discover moon cows that look like giant, armor-plated caterpillars, and a vast, crystal-formed city containing the faintly insectoid Selenites, which are governed by a figure in a bubble called the Grand Lunar. Fearing that earthlings will increasingly come to the moon and bring destruction, the Grand Lunar orders them all to remain on the moon. Cavor does, though Bedford and Callender return to Earth. However, they have no evidence of the trip, because the

space pod sinks in the ocean. Modern pictures of the ruined Selenite city cause Bedford to speculate that Cavor destroyed the moon civilization, not with the feared violence but by infecting them with his head cold.

First Men in the Moon had been a long-held dream of Ray Harryhausen that came to fruition when he convinced British sci-fi writer Nigel Kneale to do the script. A key element of the Dynamation process was to direct the live action in such a way that it corresponded with the planned effects that would be inserted later, so the merging of the two appeared seamless. The model figures would be placed on a miniature set with the live-action footage projected one frame at a time in the background. Harryhausen would move his figure and film it against the background frame, then advance the background, and reposition the figure and take another frame. It took weeks and weeks of work to produce an entire sequence in Dynamation. The key Selenite characters were animated in this fashion. Crowd scenes were shot using children standing in the background wearing Selenite costumes. For the sequence featuring the Grand Lunar, Harryhausen moved a distortion glass with each frame exposure, which imbued the bubble with a rippling effect. What he was most proud of, however, was the opening sequence, in which the modern moon mission was created with as much accuracy as possible, thanks to NASA's compliance with a request for spacecraft designs and information.

At the time, one actor's appearance in the film went unnoticed: Peter Finch, who was then at the height of his stardom, wandered onto the First Men in the Moon soundstage at Shepperton Studios in England from an adjoining set, and was pressed into service to play the bit role of a messenger after the original actor had canceled out.

**Robinson Crusoe on Mars**

**"You gotta face the reality of being alone forever."**

While the title of this cult classic might make this film sound like a Saturday morning adventure aimed at a youthful audience, Robinson Crusoe on Mars (1964) was actually intended to be a serious updating of the classic Daniel Defoe novel about a castaway struggling to survive on a deserted island, with the action transferred to a distant planet. "This film is scientifically authentic," the ads declared. "It is only one step ahead of present reality!" While that may have been an exaggeration, the film does effectively dramatize the problem of how an astronaut could cope with a long, perhaps even infinite, period of solitude in space.

The world's first two-man (and one woolly monkey) space probe heading for Mars is forced to make an emergency crash landing on the surface of Mars in order to escape a collision with a fireball, killing one man in the attempt. Astronaut Kit Draper (Paul Mantee) is forced to face the hostile planet on his own, save for Mona the Monkey. This vision of Mars has weather extremes: fire pits on the surface, vicious snowstorms, and other dangers such as a river of lava created when a flaming asteroid collides with the planet's polar ice cap. Draper does manage to find water and discovers that strange yellow rocks emit oxygen when burned, but his biggest obstacle is solitude.

After months of a solitary existence, Draper sees another ship landing. However, this ship is from an alien world located in the constellation of Orion. The alien civilization employs slave labor to mine resources on Mars. One of the slaves (Victor Lundin) escapes and joins Draper in his lonely vigil, and is, of course, dubbed "Friday." Eventually, a new mission from Earth rescues both castaways and the monkey.

A couple veterans of Martian cinema were behind the camera of Robinson Crusoe on Mars: Danish-born Ib Melchior, whose last trip to Mars was 1959's Angry Red Planet, co-wrote the screenplay with John C. Higgins, while Byron Haskin, who directed Pal's The

*Above: "Cinemagic," which was used to film scenes of Angry Red Planet, was a system for making live action look faintly like animation. It was developed by cartoonist Norman Maurer.*

*Opposite top: A charmingly quaint Victorian space capsule from The First Men in the Moon.*

*Opposite bottom: Castaway Paul Mantee in Robinson Crusoe on Mars.*

*War of the Worlds*, took the reins here as well. Many of the Mars scenes were filmed in California's desolate Death Valley, a convincing stand-in for the surface of Mars, particularly when an orange-red sky was composited into the shot through optical effects. The cast budget for *Robinson Crusoe on Mars* must have set a record for the least amount ever spent on a major studio film. Aside from Mantee and Lundin, there was only one other major speaking role, that of the astronaut who is killed while landing on the planet. It was played by an actor whose status as an unknown would radically change within a couple years: Adam West.

*Above left: Victor Lundin as Friday and Paul Mantee as the stranded spaceman in* Robinson Crusoe on Mars.

*Above right: Paul Mantee's only other companion while stranded on Mars in* Robinson Crusoe on Mars *was Mona the Monkey.*

## Lost in Space
### "Danger! Danger, Will Robinson!"

While the literary source for *Robinson Crusoe on Mars* was obvious, the one for the television series *Lost in Space* was not, unless one knew the title under which the show was developed: *Space Family Robinson*. It was the brainchild of producer Irwin Allen, who had won an Oscar in 1952 for Best Documentary for *The Sea Around Us* and went on to produce the sci-fi films *The Lost World* (1960), *Voyage to the Bottom of the Sea* (1961), which became a series in 1964, and *Five Weeks in a Balloon* (1962).

*Lost in Space*, which premiered on CBS in 1965, depicts the Robinson family of astronauts: parents John and Maureen (Guy Williams and June Lockhart), teenager Judy (Marta Kristen), adolescent Penny (Angela Cartwright), and young whiz kid Will (Billy Mumy). Their mission aboard the *Jupiter II* is to travel to a planet orbiting Alpha Centauri, the star nearest the sun, in hopes of colonizing it. Joining Professor Robinson and his family are the pilot, Major Don West (Mark Goddard), a verbose robot with no name (officially it's a Class M-3 Model B9, General Utility Non-Theorizing Environmental Control Robot), and Dr. Zachary Smith (Jonathan Harris). Smith is not supposed to be participating in the mission at all; he is really a foreign spy assigned by his homeland to sabotage the flight (and while his country is never disclosed, viewers of the time could reasonably assume his allegiance was to the Soviets). He does manage to reprogram the mission, but in the process gets trapped on board so that when the *Jupiter II* is thrown off course, Smith is thrown with it.

*Above left*: The cast of Lost in Space: the robot, June Lockhart, Guy Williams, Marta Kristen, Don Goddard, Billy Mumy, Jonathan Harris, and Angela Cartwright.

*Above right*: After the first season of Lost in Space, the series filmed in color.

*Left*: With time, the storylines and the acting style for Lost in Space leaned heavily toward broad comedy.

**Top**: *The Jupiter II from television's* Lost in Space.

**Above**: *Jack Johnson as Will Robinson operating a very different sort of robot from the 1998 feature film version of* Lost in Space.

When the program began it was in black and white and presented a more or less realistic sci-fi family adventure. Very quickly, however, Dr. Smith and the robot emerged as the real stars of the series, so episodes became tailored around them. Harris began playing Smith for comedy, pushing the character far closer to Mr. Belvedere than Dr. No, and the robot became one of the iconic figures in 1960s. Only Billy Mumy was able to hold his own against Harris and the robot (played by stuntman Bob May in the suit, and given voice by announcer Dick Tufeld), becoming a kind of foil for their antics. Starting with the second season, the show was filmed in color, and the Robinson family seemed not so much lost as on an extended intergalactic vacation, visiting strange planets with even stranger creatures, everything from a space pirate to a giant carrot. The latter, from the episode "The Great Vegetable Rebellion," was the high point of inanity for the program, if not for television in general.

*Lost in Space* left the air in 1968, as did Allen's series spin-off *Voyage to the Bottom of the Sea*, another show that started out more or less serious but became increasingly absurd with time. (The same creature costumes would often appear on both.) Allen also produced *The Time Tunnel* (1966–67), about two young scientists who were caught in a perpetual government-induced time warp, and *Land of the Giants* (1968–70), about a spaceship that crashes onto a mysterious world where everybody is seventy feet tall. In the 1970s Allen would reinvent himself as "The Master of Disaster," the purveyor of such epics as *The Poseidon Adventure* (1972) and *The Towering Inferno* (1974).

*Lost in Space* was remade for the big screen in 1998, a version that was far less wacky than the TV show and carried an ecological message. Original cast members June Lockhart, Don Goddard, Marta Kristen, and Angela Cartwright made cameo appearances in the film. The remake earned headlines for being the film to knock *Titanic* out of the number-one box office spot after its four-month reign.

**Above left**: *This giant cyclops was one of the most memorable creatures encountered by the Robinson family on* Lost in Space. *It even inspired the plastic model kit based on the series.*

**Top**: *Richard Basehart (left) and David Hedison played the highest ranking officers aboard the submarine* Seaview *on television's* Voyage to the Bottom of the Sea.

**Above**: *The time travel device from TV's* The Time Tunnel.

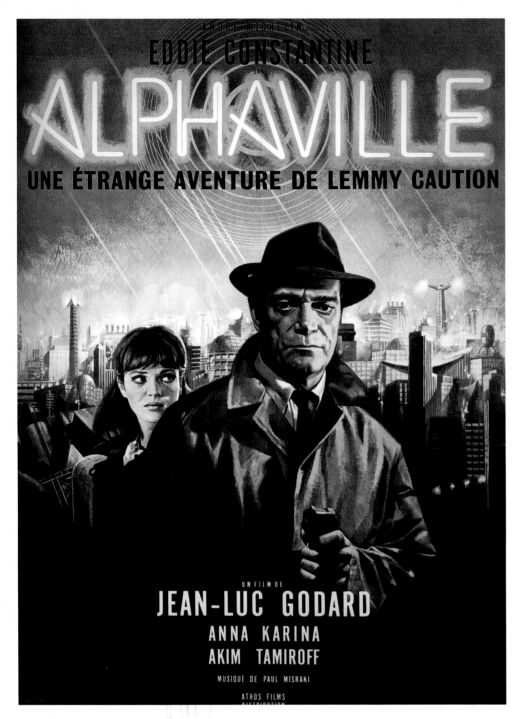

A·N·D·R·E··M·I·C·H·E·L·I·N····

EDDIE CONSTANTINE

DANS

ALPHAVILLE

UNE ÉTRANGE AVENTURE DE LEMMY CAUTION

UN FILM DE

JEAN-LUC GODARD

ANNA KARINA

AKIM TAMIROFF

MUSIQUE DE PAUL MISRAKI

ATHOS FILMS
DISTRIBUTION

*Above*: Alphaville *was director Jean-Luc Godard's homage to the American noir B-films of the 1940s.*

*Opposite top*: Eddie Constantine leading with his gun as P.I. Lemmy Caution.

*Opposite bottom*: Lemmy Caution (Eddie Constantine) peruses the sinister image of Professor von Braun (Howard Vernon), the creator of the city, in Alphaville.

### Alphaville
**"All things weird are normal in this whore of cities."**

*Alphaville* (1965), a strange, disturbing, dystopian adventure made by French New Wave director Jean-Luc Godard, is the first example of noirpunk, a film that combines a futuristic setting and the sensibilities of a 1940s crime drama. The lead character of *Alphaville* is Lemmy Caution, a private eye created in 1936 by author Peter Cheyney. Caution had already appeared in a few French films, each time played by American-born-singer-turned-French-film-star Eddie Constantine. The concept of a popular trench-coated P.I. in a futuristic world was quite a leap of faith for audiences, but not for Godard, who dedicated *Alphaville* (which is accurately subtitled *A Strange Adventure of Lemmy Caution*) to PRC (Producer's Releasing Corporation), the studio behind the surrealistic, 1945 no-budget classic *Detour*.

Alphaville is the name of a grim, futuristic city where base needs, including physical needs, are catered to, but genuine love and affection have been banned. The city is completely controlled by a computer brain called Alpha 60, which was created by Professor Leonard Nosferatu, who also goes by the name of von Braun. World-weary gumshoe Lemmy Caution is dispatched from the Outlands to the city in order to locate a missing agent. He is also tasked with finding von Braun and forcing him to abdicate as ruler of Alphaville; if he fails, Caution must kill him and destroy Alpha 60. Caution achieves his first two assignments, but in the process meets and falls in love with von Braun's daughter Natacha (Anna Karina), who works as a programmer for Alpha 60. Caution ultimately short-circuits the computer brain by reciting poetry to it, thus bringing the city to a grinding halt.

Stark, ugly, and violent, *Alphaville* confounds viewers even today. It has a bizarre sense of humor that manifests in the film's character names—Professor von Braun, née Nosferatu, is named after both the German rocket scientist Werner von Braun and the German cinema's silent version of *Dracula*, while a couple scientists in the film are named "Heckell" and "Jeckell" after the cartoon magpies. With the sound off, it looks like any other low-budget crime drama; only the dialogue reveals it to be a futuristic story. The film's interior sets are drab and sterile, and the exteriors are all buildings in Paris that existed at the time but shot in such a way, often at dusk or after dark, that the structures look futuristic and intimidating. The film was shot on 16mm, further giving it a harsh, grainy look. Subsequent noirpunk films that followed *Alphaville*, notably *Blade Runner*, would take far more care in defining their retro-futuristic world—but *Alphaville* was the one that blazed the trail.

**Above**: Anna Karina and Eddie Constantine in Alphaville, *which offered a cacophony of visual styles.*

**Right**: *Eddie Constantine, director Jean-Luc Godard, and Anna Karina on the set of Alphaville.*

**Above**: Cyril Cusack (left) and Oskar Werner
warm themselves over burning pages in
Fahrenheit 451.

### Fahrenheit 451

*"The only way to be happy is for everyone to be made equal. So, we must burn the
books."*

Like *1984* and *Brave New World*, *Fahrenheit 451*—"the temperature at which book
paper catches fire and burns"—has become a science fiction brand name. Based on an earlier short story called "The Fireman," Ray Bradbury's 1953 novel was set in a world where
books are declared dangerous and not only banned but burned if they are discovered
anywhere. Bradbury's vision of the future also included firemen who start fires instead of
extinguish them, a mechanical firehouse dog, and a world governed by wall-sized television
screens, which preclude any form of reading.

The film version of *Fahrenheit 451*, released in 1966, featured only normal-sized televi-
sions and no mechanical dog but capitalized on images of block-housing units in England,
whose utter uniformity appears futuristic, and shots of a sleek monorail that was not a model
but an actual working, if experimental, train in Loiret, France. The only true futuristic props,
except for the austere-looking fire trucks, were the rocket packs worn by the firemen. In this
world where books are outlawed so that conformity may reign, fireman Guy Montag (Oskar
Werner) becomes curious about books after a chance meeting with a neighbor, Clarisse
(Julie Christie). Clarisse believes the rumor that once upon a time, firemen put out fires. Guy
becomes a secret reader but is turned in to authorities by his wife Linda (also played by Julie
Christie) and assigned to burn his own book collection. Instead, he immolates the fire chief
(Cyril Cusack) and escapes to the settlement of the "book people"—a group that includes

THE SCIENCE FICTION UNIVERSE . . . AND BEYOND

*Right: Julie Christie as Linda, the television-absorbed wife of Montag, in Fahrenheit 451.*

*Bottom right: Ray Bradbury, the author of Fahrenheit 451.*

*Opposite top left: A librarian chooses to die with her books in Fahrenheit 451.*

*Opposite top right: Even though the monorail was real, it lent a futuristic touch to Fahrenheit 451.*

*Opposite bottom: The fire unit from Fahrenheit 451.*

Clarisse—who have each memorized a book in order to preserve it. Meanwhile, in order to save face over Montag's rebellion, the government televises his "capture"—actually a staged act involving a double—leaving Montag free to live with the book people.

*Fahrenheit 451* was French director Francois Truffaut's only English-language film, but interestingly enough, he spoke no English himself at that time. Werner, Christie, and cinematographer Nicholas Roeg all spoke French on the set, though in Werner's case it became moot when he and Truffaut stopped speaking at all. They feuded over the actor's quirky interpretation of the role, which Truffaut felt should be more "robotic," given the nature of the story. In retaliation, Werner purposefully cut his hair one night so Truffaut's shots would not match. Interestingly, the studio behind the film, Universal, was squeamish about the scenes actually showing books going up in a bonfire; they requested that Truffaut use only works in the public domain. Truffaut declined, and as an in-joke, the burned works include copies of the French film magazine *Cahiers du Cinéma*, which had published Truffaut's reviews before he turned to filmmaking.

While Ray Bradbury was happy with this adaptation of his book, not all Bradbury-inspired films have fared as well (1969's *The Illustrated Man*, for instance). In 1985 the author was able to take matters into his own hands by co-producing and scripting each episode of *The Ray Bradbury Theater*, an anthology series based on his stories. The series ran to acclaim for six seasons, with original episodes airing first on HBO and later on the USA Network.

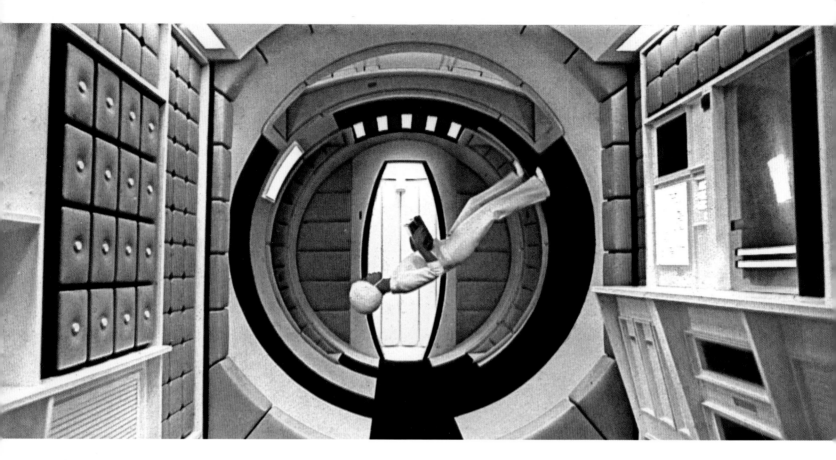

# "Just what do you think you're doing, Dave?"

There are scores of people today who will go to their graves still outraged that *Oliver!*, the bombastic, glossy, over-produced film version of the London musical adaptation of Dickens's *Oliver Twist*, won the 1968 Academy Award for Best Picture, while Stanley Kubrick's *2001: A Space Odyssey* was not even nominated.

Perhaps the quintessential science fiction epic of its era, *2001* has lost little of its power over the past four decades. But neither has it gained much in the way of our understanding of its enigmatic ending. The story concerns the discovery of a strange monolith on the moon—one that appears to have influenced life on Earth since the dawn of mankind—which is emitting signals to Jupiter. The spaceship *Discovery*, carrying astronauts Dave Bowman (Keir Dullea) and Frank Poole (Gary Lockwood), is dispatched to Jupiter in hopes of figuring out what is going on. Their mission is ultimately sabotaged by a too-smart computer brain named HAL 9000 (voiced by Douglas Rain). By the film's end, only Bowman survives,

though the evolutionary stage in which he ends up remains something of a puzzle.

Directed by Kubrick from the script he wrote with Arthur C. Clarke, *2001: A Space Odyssey* began filming in late 1965. It was originally scheduled for release in 1967 but held back, ostensibly to finish the effects but most likely due to Kubrick's obsessive perfectionism. Much of the press attention at the time was devoted to the "centrifuge," a revolving wheel thirty-eight feet in diameter that had been built to rotate at a rate of three miles an hour, allowing actor Lockwood to jog on it like a treadmill while the camera and cameraman rotated on a gimbal system around him. This was not a new technique—Fred Astaire danced up the wall and on the ceiling in *Royal Wedding* (1951) using the same means—but the outer space setting made the effect look all the more convincing. Similarly, Kubrick and his effects team used the time-honored technique of hooking actors to wires and flying them to simulate weightlessness. They kept the wires from being visible in an

**Right**: *Keir Dullea as astronaut Dave Bowman in* 2001: A Space Odyssey.

**Opposite**: *Shots in* 2001: A Space Odyssey. *such as this, in which Edwina Carroll takes a zero-gravity walk, were created by locking the camera to a rotating set.*

**Above**: *Co-writer/producer/director Stanley Kubrick on the set of* 2001: A Space Odyssey.

ingenious way: the "weightless" actors were always dropping toward the camera, which was on the floor inside a vertically built set, so that the wires attached to their backs were hidden by their bodies.

The real special-effects innovation of *2001*, however, was invisible to the eye: the use of front projection. Nearly all films up to that point utilized rear projection, in which scenery was projected onto a screen behind the actors. Kubrick and special-effects supervisor Tom Howard developed a front projection system through which an eight-by-ten-inch transparency could be projected *over* the actors onto a highly reflective screen behind them, creating an absolutely convincing background. The parts of the transparency that landed on the actor weren't visible on camera; this was the process used for the "Dawn of Man" sequence. Front projection was also employed to create the image of astro-nauts inside the rocket ship. The model rocket ship with its windows blacked out was moved past the camera on a track, and

then returned to its first position. Then it made another pass in front of the camera, only this time the model was covered with a black cloth with only the highly reflective windows visible. A small projector running on a synchronized track cast the images of the actors onto the windows, making it look as though they were inside. The result-ing film contained both images, printed together as a double exposure.

The impact of *2001* is difficult to over-state, and not simply for its Oscar-winning special effects. Kubrick's use of Richard Strauss's *Thus Spoke Zarathustra* created a classic moment on film that has been end-lessly parodied. And regarding that theory that the computer is named HAL because either Arthur C. Clarke or Kubrick felt that the *real* menace of the twentieth century was an actual company, whose name is made up of letters one alphabet letter advanced from H, A, and L, respectively? Both Kubrick and Clarke dismissed it as an urban legend.

Some of the more puzzling questions posed by *2001* were cleared up in its 1984

sequel, *2010*, directed by Peter Hyams. In this film, a joint U.S./U.S.S.R. mission travels to Jupiter aboard the Soviet ship *Alexei Leonov* to recover the derelict *Discovery*, the spaceship from the original movie. On board is Dr. Heywood Flood (played by Roy Scheider; in *2001* William Sylvester took the role), who was scapegoated for the failure of *Discovery*'s mission and the deaths (real or perceived) of her crew. Finding the *Discovery* operational, the new crew gets it running again, and even powers up HAL 9000, who, it is learned, was secretly programmed by governmental forces back on Earth to lie to Bowman and Poole about their real mission, which was to investigate the mysterious monolith. HAL malfunctioned trying to process the conflicting orders.

Even though the United States and the Soviet Union are close to hostilities back home, the joint American and Soviet crew has to work together to avoid being destroyed by the power of the monolith, which is transforming Jupiter into a new star. This causes Jupiter's moon Europa to become habitable, though Bowman—who is now at one with the monolith—reappears to warn the earthlings not to colonize Europa but instead leave it for another race. This message is received on Earth, and peace is reached.

*2010* was an early example of filmmakers using digital imagery in its special effects. The thousands of monoliths that envelop Jupiter and transform it into a star were created with computers. But the film's real distinction may be that it accurately predicted that the United States and the Soviet Union would some day unite for a joint space mission. In 1984, when the film was made, *that* idea was as much science fiction as traveling to Jupiter.

**Above**: *Missing links discover the monolith in* 2001: A Space Odyssey.

**Left**: *A sample of the groundbreaking special effects supervised by Douglas Trumbull for* 2001: A Space Odyssey.

**Top**: Astronauts Poole (Gary Lockwood) and Bowman (Keir Dullea) on board ship in 2001: A Space Odyssey.

**Above**: Bowman reborn for the enigmatic ending of 2001: A Space Odyssey.

With each and every NASA space launch of the 1960s, leading up to the monumentally historic moon landing in August of 1969, science fiction came closer to being science fact. Simply showing astronauts on a rocket ship on a theoretical mission to the moon or a planet was no longer enough to entice moviegoers into theaters or fix eyeballs onto a television screen. Sci-fi now had to be about something. Films of this era increasingly raised issues of consciousness, overpopulation, anxiety about the speed of technological advancement, questions of humanity, and increasingly, ecology. (Of course, there are always exceptions, notably 1968's *Barbarella*, which was essentially a swinging-sixties *Playboy* photo spread with an otherworldly backdrop committed to film.) The amazement was still there, of course, but the best of sci-fi now made its audience think as well.

**Above**: *Raquel Welch and Stephen Boyd are all business in* Fantastic Voyage.

**Opposite top**: *One of the elaborate—if fanciful— sets representing the interior of the human body in* Fantastic Voyage.

**Opposite bottom**: Fantastic Voyage's *micro- miniaturized crew escapes from the body of a comatose scientist (Jan Del Val) inside a teardrop.*

### Fantastic Voyage
#### "But I don't want to be miniaturized!"

By 1966, audiences had seen just about every variation of a manned craft launched into outer space. In *Fantastic Voyage*, one of the most highly hyped sci-fi films of its time, the goal was to explore *inner* space—more specifically, inside the human body. Its plot parallels the technology race then going on between the United States and the Soviet Union, though here, the finish line is not the conquest of space but the ability to shrink objects and humans to microscopic size on a permanent basis. A Soviet bloc scientist named Jan Benes has developed such technology, while American scientists have only been able to miniaturize things for a limited amount of time. Aided by CIA agent Grant (Stephen Boyd), Benes tries to defect to the West but is thwarted by an assassination attempt, which leaves him with a blood clot in his brain. Grant and a team of scientists and technicians board a submarine called the *Proteus*, which is shrunk to atomic size and injected into Benes's body. Their mission is to find and remove the clot. However, there are two complications: one is that they have only an hour before they revert to normal size, and the other is that one of the crew is a double agent, assigned to foil the mission. Well, *three* complications, if you count the fact that an all-male crew is confined aboard the *Proteus* with a jumpsuited Raquel Welch.

Once the mission is underway, *Fantastic Voyage* plays like most other sci-fi adventures, except the dangers here are not space monsters, aliens, or asteroids but body functions, organs, and lava-lamp-like blood flows. One massive set, simulating the inside of the lung, was built so the walls could move in and out with each "breath." Another set,

representing the interior of the brain, was crafted from fiberglass sprayed in geometric patterns. Mores of the time dictated that the sets of body parts be more imaginative and representational than realistically gooey (a consideration that would likely not be given much thought today). For sequences of the crew swimming in blood streams, the actors were filmed dry, flying on wires, and the action was filmed with the camera running three times faster than normal, which served to slow down the action on screen. Ironically, the *Proteus*, which in the film was a micrometer long, was in many scenes a full-sized mock-up, measuring forty-two feet long.

The director and production designer of *Fantastic Voyage* were Richard Fleischer and Harper Goff, respectively, who had previously joined forces on *20,000 Leagues Under the Sea*, which also featured a high-tech sub. And like the earlier film, *Fantastic Voyage* also experienced wire problems: in some shots of the actors "swimming," the cables holding them aloft are highly visible.

*Above*: Raquel Welch is ready for action in Fantastic Voyage.

*Opposite top*: Floating around inside a lung in Fantastic Voyage.

*Opposite bottom*: The aliens' plan to land on Earth completely unseen doesn't quite work, creating problems for witness Roy Thinnes, in TV's The Invaders.

## The Invaders

***"Now David Vincent knows that the Invaders are here. . . . Somehow, he must convince a disbelieving world that the nightmare has begun."***

Television's *The Invaders*, which premiered in 1967, was an adult-oriented science fiction series that aired at a time when many of the other sci-fi adventure shows, such as *Lost in Space* and *Voyage to the Bottom of the Sea*, capitalized on broader, more outlandish stories and characters. The aliens in *The Invaders* remained unidentified throughout the series—at least as far as their planet origins are concerned—but they have come to Earth with the intent of taking it over. They are able to disguise themselves as regular humans, except for one strange visual quirk: weirdly bent pinkie fingers that they cannot move. They also can't bleed, but one has to shoot them before finding that out. Unlike other paranoia-themed sci-fi films, *The Invaders* offered a new wrinkle: not only does hero David Vincent (Roy Thinnes), an architect who stumbles across the landing of the spaceship one dark night, know that the Invaders are here, but *they* know he knows, which causes him to go on the run. *The Invaders* was a purposeful attempt by its producer, the prolific Quinn Martin, to meld the sci-fi/paranoia genre with the man-on-the-run format of his most successful television series, *The Fugitive*.

At the beginning of the series, which ran on ABC, Vincent is completely alone in his quest to stop the encroachment of the aliens and convince others of the danger. The authorities are often seen as unwitting accomplices to the Invaders; at other times, the authorities *are* the Invaders who managed to infiltrate the police force. It is not only possible to kill the aliens with conventional weapons, it is also fairly easy. But because their bodies disintegrate instantly upon death, it is as though they had never been there, and Vincent is left without any verifiable proof for his claims. In time he is able to convince a

**Top left**: Roy Thinnes, as David Vincent, was on a two-season quest to obtain proof of the aliens' presence in The Invaders.

**Top right**: Humans being "preserved" for later use by the Invaders.

**Above left**: The aliens looked like this when they were shot in The Invaders.

**Above right**: The Invaders' *spaceship*.

*Above*: Patrick McGoohan as "Number 6" campaigns to become Number 2 in The Prisoner.

few other recurring characters that the invasion is underway, and in one instance even encounters a mutant Invader who feels sympathy for him. But none of that mattered much; by the time the series left the air, Vincent was still on the run.

The special-effects budget for *The Invaders* remained low, because the primary effects were the red, glowing auras given to the mortally wounded aliens, who would then turn into piles of dust. The ratings for the series also remained relatively low, which prompted producer Martin to go back to crime dramas. But the lone-man-with-a-secret-wandering-from-the-authorities angle would be put to good use on TV a decade later in the series *The Incredible Hulk*.

### The Prisoner
#### "I am not a number. I am a person!"

*The Prisoner*, produced in England in 1967 and exported to the United States the following year, was the perfect entertainment for those who thought that Stanley Kubrick had over-explained things in *2001: A Space Odyssey*. It was created by Irish actor Patrick McGoohan, who starred and executive produced the series and wrote and directed many of the 17 episodes. *The Prisoner* presented a Kafkaesque nightmare prompted by the resignation of a British secret agent, who is immediately abducted and taken to a strange, conformist, but outwardly pleasant place called the Village, where he takes up residence as Number 6. Almost everyone at the Village goes by a number instead of a name. Naturally, Number 1 is the person in charge, but it is his lieutenant, Number 2, who is most frequently seen and who interacts with Number 6. Number 6 eventually learns from the various Number 2s ("Number 2" changes throughout the course of the series for various reasons) that he has been brought to the Village because of the information he carries around in his head, and the fact that he resigned so summarily. The implication is Number 1 does not want whatever Number 6 knows to fall into the hands of the enemy . . . if indeed Number 1 is not already the enemy.

Each episode of *The Prisoner* focused on Number 6's attempts to either escape from the Village, where every room is either bugged or might be bugged, or find out the exact nature of his imprisonment. In one episode, "Free for All," he even runs in an election for the post of Number 2, but finds it no more to his liking than his position as Number 6. While the series was always compelling, very few answers were provided until the very end of the show's run. Then it was revealed that Number 6 is really John Drake, the lead character of

*Opposite top*: A genuine human chess game represents the metaphoric chess game of Number 6's attempts to discover the secret of the Village in TV's The Prisoner.

*Opposite bottom*: The Prisoner's *bizarre surrealism resulted in the show's becoming a cult hit. Star Patrick McGoohan (left) also created the series.*

McGoohan's prior series, *Secret Agent*, and most shocking of all, *he* is Number 1, trapped within the confines of his own psyche. He is allowed to escape the Village physically . . . but mentally?

The small Welsh village of Portmeirion, which possesses a visual cacophony of different architectural styles, served as the exterior of the Village. *The Prisoner*, which aired on CBS, appeared at a time when the success of *The Avengers* made American television safe for other British-made sci-fi or quasi-sci-fi series, including *The Champions* (1968), a shorter-lived show about a trio of secret agents who developed superpowers in Tibet.

Themes of conformity and "fighting the system," as well as the psychedelic production style and trippy visuals, resonated with a 1960s audience and the show is now remembered as a genuine cult classic. A new version of the story was made for American cable TV in 2009, as a six-part miniseries starring Jim Caviezel and Ian McKellen. That version did not have the same impact in the marketplace, most likely due to its themes being somewhat less relevant to much of today's audience.

### THX 1138

#### *"You have nowhere to go. You have nowhere to go."*

In 1971, years before he created the adventurous *Star Wars*, George Lucas presented one of the bleakest visions of the future ever put on film in *THX 1138*. Patterned heavily after George Orwell's seminal dystopian vision *1984* (which has been filmed several times, but never definitively), *THX 1138* depicts a sterile twenty-fifth-century world where individuality is completely subsumed by the state. People wear identical white suits, they all have androgynous shaved heads, and instead of names, they go by alphanumeric codes. There is no sex, love is considered the "ultimate perversion," and everyone is medicated into submission so there are no emotions and therefore no emotional problems. Corporations are in charge, consumerism is promoted, and state-sponsored surveillance is the norm. Then a woman named LUH 3417 (Maggie McOmie) decides to rebel and stop taking her meds. She gets her roommate THX 1138 (Robert Duvall) to stop as well. This releases his emotions, and the two end up in a torrid affair. After they are caught engaging in the "ultimate perversion," they are sent to a stark-white, featureless prison room. THX 1138 and another prisoner eventually escape. (That prisoner, SEN 5241, was played by Donald Pleasence, who before becoming immortalized as Dr. Loomis in the *Halloween* series was one of the more ubiquitous faces and voices of 1960s and '70s sci-fi.) LUH does not escape. Pursued through a tunnel by the very steel-faced android policemen that THX helped to build, he manages to get away completely. He realizes for the first time that civilization as he knows it actually exists underground. He climbs to the surface of the Earth as a new day dawns— literally and figuratively.

Shot in 1969, *THX 1138* was an expansion of a fifteen-minute film *THX 1138:4EB*, which Lucas had made two years earlier while a film student at the University of Southern California. After the commercial version was released, the short was retitled *Electronic Labyrinth* so as to avoid confusion. *THX 1138* was shot in the San Francisco area, which

*Above top*: Number 6 isn't having a ball *attempting to escape in* The Prisoner.

*Above*: The robotic police of George Lucas's THX 1138 *could be seen as dry runs for the Storm Troopers of Star Wars.*

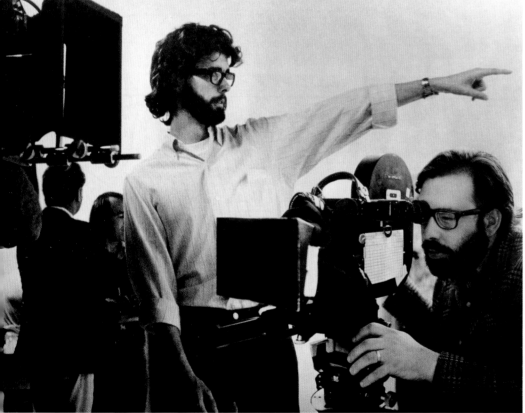

**Top**: THX 1138 (Robert Duvall) is held at bay in the White Limbo prison of THX 1138.

**Above left**: Writer/director George Lucas (pointing) and executive producer Francis Ford Coppola on the set of THX 1138.

**Above right**: Winston Smith (John Hurt) and Julia (Suzanna Hamilton) dare to love in the future in 1984 (1984).

Visit the future where love
is the ultimate crime.

# THX 1138

Warner Bros. presents THX 1138 · An American Zoetrope Production · Starring Robert Duvall and Donald Pleasence · with Don Pedro Colley, Maggie McOmie and Ian Wolfe · Technicolor® · Techniscope® · Executive Producer, Francis Ford Coppola · Screenplay by George Lucas and Walter Murch · Story by George Lucas Produced by Lawrence Sturhahn · Directed by George Lucas · Music by Lalo Schifrin

FROM Warner bros. A Kinney company [GP]

is where executive producer Francis Ford Coppola had his home base, and it used actual locations wherever possible, such as Posey Tube, the Caldicott Tunnel, and a then-unfinished Bay Area Rapid Transit tunnel, inside which Lucas staged the climactic car and motorcycle chase scene. Maggie McOmie was chosen over two hundred other actresses for the role of LUH but failed to parlay the experience into a subsequent film career. Upon its release the film was criticized for having a derivative, dull script, written by Lucas and Walter Murch, but it won praise for its striking visuals and for Murch's sound design. Instead of using stock sound effects from an existing library, Murch recorded distinctive sounds for the film. Sound was such an important element in this film that Lucas named his digital sound system THX.

### The Andromeda Strain
***"Most of them died instantly. A few had time to go quietly nuts."***

In *The War of the Worlds* the alien invaders were vanquished by earthly bacteria and viruses, to which they had no immunity. Ditto the Selenites of *First Men in the Moon.* Maybe *The Andromeda Strain* was the extraterrestrials' revenge; the premise is that a global species is threatened by deadly microorganisms, but in this case the species is us. Based on the best-selling novel by Michael Crichton, *The Andromeda Strain* (1971) follows a team of government troubleshooters who are dispatched to New Mexico, the landing spot of a fallen satellite that was part of the top-secret SCOOP project studying the potential for biological warfare. The satellite's mission was to glean space microbes, and practically everyone within proximity of the satellite is either dead or dying. Once the craft is brought to an underground laboratory called Wildfire, the team discovers that a deadly space microbe was carried to Earth with the craft. They also discover that the organism, dubbed Andromeda, mutates so rapidly that it cannot be counteracted before its next mutation. As

*Above*: THX 1138 *drew its inspiration from George Orwell's* 1984.

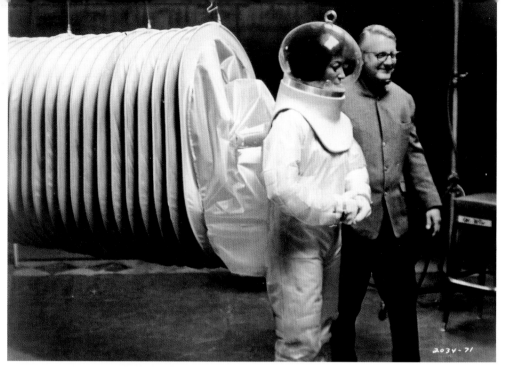

*Above*: These aren't astronauts on another planet, but scientists in HazMat suits in The Andromeda Strain.

*Right top*: Paula Kelly with director Robert Wise on the set of The Andromeda Strain.

*Right*: James Olson examines those immune to the deadly space bacteria while Paula Kelly looks on in The Andromeda Strain.

they struggle to find an antidote for the space virus, a deadly countdown begins due to the security program built into the Wildfire facility: it will self-destruct via a nuclear device if a major threat to the facility's security is detected. Andromeda poses precisely that threat, unless the scientists can stop it.

Billed as the story of "the world's first space-age crisis," *The Andromeda Strain* is a very realistic and tech-savvy science fiction movie. There are no rockets, no aliens as such, and there are no foreign governments posing a threat. If anything, the picture, directed by Robert Wise (*The Day the Earth Stood Still*), points a finger in the mirror; the film implies that we could be the means of our own destruction in the name of biological research. Since the antagonist is a virus, the film is more clinical than spectacular; in fact, its chief special effect is the graphic depiction of the microbe's rapid mutation and growth.

*The Andromeda Strain* was remade as a miniseries for the A&E Network in 2008, and this version contained a twist: it is suspected that a future Earth society sent the microbe into the past through a wormhole—meaning that it arrives in the present—as their only means of getting rid of it!

**Above**: James Olson in The Andromeda Strain. The film's sense of reality was enhanced by using actors who were not major stars for the lead roles.

**Right**: While clearly not in good shape, Jackson (George Mitchell, right) is one of only two people who don't die from the space microbe in The Andromeda Strain.

Amazing companions on an incredible adventure...that journeys beyond imagination!

When in Southern California visit Universal Studios

# "silent running"

**starring**

# Bruce Dern · with Cliff Potts · Ron Rifkin · Jesse Vint

Original Songs Sung by | Original Music Composed and Conducted by | Written by | Directed by

JOAN BAEZ · PETER SCHICKELE · DERIC WASHBURN & MIKE CIMINO and STEVE BOCHCO · Douglas TRUMBULL

Produced by MICHAEL GRUSKOFF · A MICHAEL GRUSKOFF / DOUGLAS TRUMBULL PRODUCTION

A UNIVERSAL RELEASE · TECHNICOLOR® · G ALL AGES ADMITTED General Audiences · ORIGINAL SOUNDTRACK ALBUM NOW AVAILABLE EXCLUSIVELY ON DECCA RECORDS

### Silent Running

***"We have just received orders to abandon and nuclear destruct all the forests."***

*Silent Running*—the wartime term for a submarine running in quiet, undetectable mode—is considered by some to be the first science fiction film with an overt ecological message, namely that once the forests and the trees are gone, they are gone for good. Reinforcing the film's "message picture" status was the fact that folksinger Joan Baez contributed songs to the film's soundtrack.

Released in 1972, *Silent Running* is set in a future world where plant life has become extinct on the surface of the Earth, and the last vestiges of it are contained in enormous hothouse domes connected to spaceships in orbit. The goal is that some day, the plants will be brought back to reforest the Earth. Orders come from Earth to destroy the domes so that the spacecraft can be returned to commercial service. Most of the crewmen aboard the spaceship *Valley Forge* don't care about the plants and simply want to go home, but botanist Freeman Lowell (Bruce Dern) cares deeply. He rebels and ends up killing some of his crewmates in order to save the plants. He has help in the form of three small robotic drones named Huey, Dewey, and Louie, who, while not humanoid in appearance, have distinct personalities.

*Silent Running* was the first picture directed by special-effects wizard Douglas Trumbull, who had worked with Kubrick on *2001* and created the virus mutation for *The Andromeda Strain*. He employed the front-projection system pioneered on *2001* to create the geodesic domes where the plant life exists in outer space (the plants were real; the domes were projected). The drones, Huey, Dewey, and Louie, were not created from special effects. They were costumes inhabited by four double-amputees. A Vietnam veteran double-amputee named George McCart helped design the suits, which the drone actors moved around by using their hands and arms as the robots' "legs."

While the ecological message of the film is front and center, Trumbull had another message that he hoped would resonate: despite recent memories of HAL, people should not fear technology. "One of the things I wanted to do was to show machines as a tool that can and must remain under the control of human beings, not as a lurking, malevolent force," he said at the time. But is there any sort of message to be derived from the name of Lowell's spacecraft? As it turns out, no; it was so named because the scenes set inside the spaceship were filmed in the decommissioned aircraft carrier USS *Valley Forge*.

*Above*: Bruce Dern (left) and director Douglas Trumbull on the set of Silent Running.

*Opposite*: Silent Running *was one of the first sci-fi films with a strong ecological message.*

## Soylent Green

### *"People were always rotten, but the world was beautiful."*

Set in 2022 in New York, *Soylent Green* (1973) depicts a future that is not only cursed with rampant overpopulation and unemployment but also staggering pollution. If not for a miracle food manufactured and made available by the Soylent Corporation, said to be made of ocean plankton, most of humanity would go hungry. When Simonson, the head of Soylent Corporation, is murdered, Detective Thorn (Charlton Heston) is assigned to investigate. In the executive's room, he discovers papers concerning the company that he cannot read—few can in this world, since books are no longer allowed—but Thorn's elderly, bitterly nostalgic neighbor Sol Roth (Edward G. Robinson) is literate. He begins to examine the papers. Meanwhile, Thorn is becoming a . . . well, you know . . . in the side of the governor of New York, a former associate of Simonson, who tries to shut the investigation down. Thorn refuses and becomes a marked man. By this point, Sol has examined the report. It contains the information that oceans are no longer capable of sustaining plankton. Therefore Soylent Green is made from something else: *people*. Simonson was about to reveal this, which is why he was killed. Distraught over what civilization has become, Sol opts for suicide and asks Thorn to make sure his body is disposed of so it can't be recycled as food, leaving Thorn alone to fight the government, which never wants the secret of Soylent Green revealed.

*Soylent Green* was the first film to use the word "greenhouse effect" in describing the ruination of the environment. To achieve the proper unhealthy look for the exterior scenes, which were filmed on MGM's decaying back-lot New York street, director Richard Fleischer filmed opaque, gently swirling colored water and then printed that over the footage. The overpopulation issue was starting to gain traction in the 1970s, and *Soylent Green* tapped into the zeitgeist perfectly. Like *Silent Running*, *Soylent Green* demonstrated once again how science fiction can comment on, and raise awareness of, important societal issues within the context of a speculative thriller.

Incidentally, *Soylent Green* was the last movie to be shot on the studio's historic Lot 2, which was demolished shortly after filming was completed. In the midst of filming in late 1972, a party was held on the set for Edward G. Robinson, ostensibly to celebrate the fact that *Soylent Green* was his one hundred and first film. Then California governor Ronald Reagan was among the celebrities who attended. The event was also a tacit farewell party: Robinson had privately disclosed to Charlton Heston that he was dying of cancer. Robinson died before the film was released. One other achievement of *Soylent Green* was that it set a new record for the most prints being struck: 415. Compare that with the more than *14,000* screens worldwide on which *Avatar* opened thirty-six years later!

*Top*: Charlton Heston almost discovers the secret of Soylent Green *the hard way.*

*Above*: Detective Thorn's (Charlton Heston) refusal to drop a murder case with political ramifications leads to trouble in Soylent Green.

*Above*: Soylent Green *was the last film of Hollywood legend Edward G. Robinson, who died before its release.*

*Left*: *Overpopulation leads to rioting in 2022 New York, the setting for* Soylent Green.

*Above*: Vacationer Richard Benjamin draws on robot Yul Brynner in Westworld.

*Right*: It takes a lot to get rogue robotic gunslinger Yul Brynner steamed in Westworld.

BOY, HAVE WE GOT A VACATION FOR YOU...

WESTWORLD

...Where nothing can possibly go worng !

MGM Presents "WESTWORLD" Starring YUL BRYNNER   RICHARD BENJAMIN
JAMES BROLIN · Music FRED KARLIN · Written and Directed by MICHAEL CRICHTON · Produced by PAUL N. LAZARUS III
PG PARENTAL GUIDANCE SUGGESTED   PANAVISION® METROCOLOR   MGM

## Westworld

***"Doesn't anything work around here?"***

*Silent Running* may have been conceived as a plea that not all modern machinery was bad, but 1973's *Westworld*, written and directed by Michael Crichton (*The Andromeda Strain*), took the opposing viewpoint. Its advertising tag line (with intentional misspelling) was, "Boy, have we got a vacation for you, where nothing can possible go worng." On the surface a rather cynical parody of Disneyland, *Westworld* presents Delos, a state-of-the-art, exorbitantly priced theme park for adults that encompasses three different areas: MedievalWorld, RomanWorld, and WestWorld. Each is inhabited by highly realistic robots that can offer the visitor any experience, from sex with a robot to the opportunity to murder one. But suddenly the robots, which are controlled to the nth degree by a large staff of technicians, begin defying programmed orders and actually develop wills of their own. As a result, guests are getting hurt and even killed. Not surprisingly given the title, most of the action of the picture takes place in the WestWorld section of the park, where a robotic gunslinger (Yul Brynner) becomes a deadly juggernaut against guests Blaine (James Brolin) and Martin (Richard Benjamin).

Yul Brynner's gunslinger character is at once a parody of and an homage to his character from the classic western *The Magnificent Seven*. Brynner was involved in the most startling scene in the film (for its time); lab technicians pull off his face to reveal the elaborate circuitry inside the robot's head. This was accomplished via a simple substitution of the veteran actor for a prop cast in his likeness. *Westworld* did enter the history books, however, as the first film to employ digital imagery, in which pixilated footage was used to represent the robots' point of view.

***Above****: Writer Michael Crichton made a mini-career of theme-parks-gone-wrong stories with both* Westworld *and* Jurassic Park.

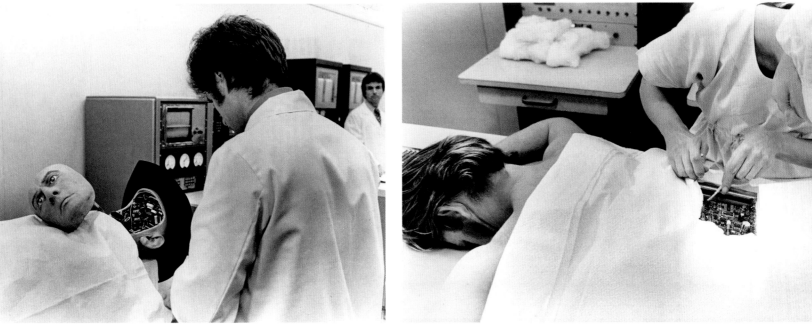

**Top**: Just because a robot can't smile doesn't mean he's not friendly, as Peter Fonda (right) learns in Futureworld.

**Above left**: This sequence of Yul Brynner's face removal was one of the most startling effects in Westworld.

**Above right**: Technicians repair the circuitry on a robotic actor in Westworld.

A sequel, *Futureworld*, came out in 1976, and this time the scientists at Delos have a genuinely nefarious plot: the theme park is a front through which world leaders will be cloned. What's more, it is discovered that the scientists running Delos are themselves robots. While *Futureworld* did not garner as much attention as its predecessor, it surpassed *Westworld* in terms of computer-generated imagery; it was the first film to feature actual digital animation as opposed to computer-enhanced graphics. The animation in question is subtle; an animated hand seen on a technician's monitor. The hand model was Dr. Ed Catmull, a pioneer in computer graphics who a few years later headed up the Graphics Group for Lucasfilm, which eventually became Pixar Animation Studios. Delos moved into television in 1980 with a series called *Beyond Westworld*, which concerned a mad scientist named Simon Quaid (James Wainwright), who wanted to use the Delos robots to take over the world and transform it into a utopia. That series lasted only five episodes on CBS.

### Rollerball

***"The game was created to demonstrate the futility of individual effort."***

The vision of the future depicted in *Rollerball* (1975), which takes place in 2018, is not one of flying cars or personal robots or bombed-out society but is eerily prophetic in its portrayal of a world where nations are obsolete and business conglomerates rule. Among them, Energy Corporation, which has hymns dedicated to it, is the most powerful. Society is based on uniformity, and materialism is believed to be the ultimate destiny of humankind. The game of Rollerball is entertainment for the masses. It's a fast, violent sport played on an oval track; players wear either roller skates or ride motorbikes. The object of the game is to catch a ball that is shot onto the track and deposit it into a goal.

Jonathan E. (James Caan) is a champion player on the so-called Energy Corp. team, based in Houston. The company, represented by chairman Mr. Bartholomew (John Houseman), is eager for him to retire. Jonathan has no intention of retiring and keeps playing, even though the games are getting more and more violent and dangerous. There is a reason for that: since Jonathan will not retire, Energy Corp. wants him to be killed. In becoming too good at the sport, Jonathan has demonstrated human potential; his individual success runs counter to Energy Corp.'s goal of using Rollerball as a way of trivializing individuality. Despite the dangers (or maybe because of them), Jonathan goes on to play one last game, which turns into a gladiatorial-style free-for-all. He manages to win, becoming a hero to the crowd because of his achievement—and Energy Corp.'s worst nightmare.

*Rollerball* was similar in theme to another film released around the same time, *Death Race 2000*. It too featured a motorized blood sport in a futuristic, totalitarian society, though it remained firmly in the exploitation camp. (*Death Race 2000* was from legendary independent producer Roger Corman and directed by cult director Paul Bartel.) Both films received an R rating, though Norman Jewison, the director of *Rollerball*, fought against this,

*Above: Racing is a blood sport in* Rollerball, *a dystopian view of the near future.*

**Above**: James Caan ("#8") keeps his eye on the ball and on the opponent trying to hurt him in Rollerball.

**Left**: The game turns increasingly deadly in Rollerball.

**Opposite top**: Director Norman Jewison was surprised by those who felt the violence in Rollerball was gratuitous, believing that he was taking a stand against violence.

**Opposite bottom left**: John Houseman as the amoral corporate executive Mr. Bartholomew in Rollerball.

**Opposite bottom right**: LL Cool J, Chris Klein, and Rebecca Romijn starred in the 2002 remake of Rollerball, set in the present day.

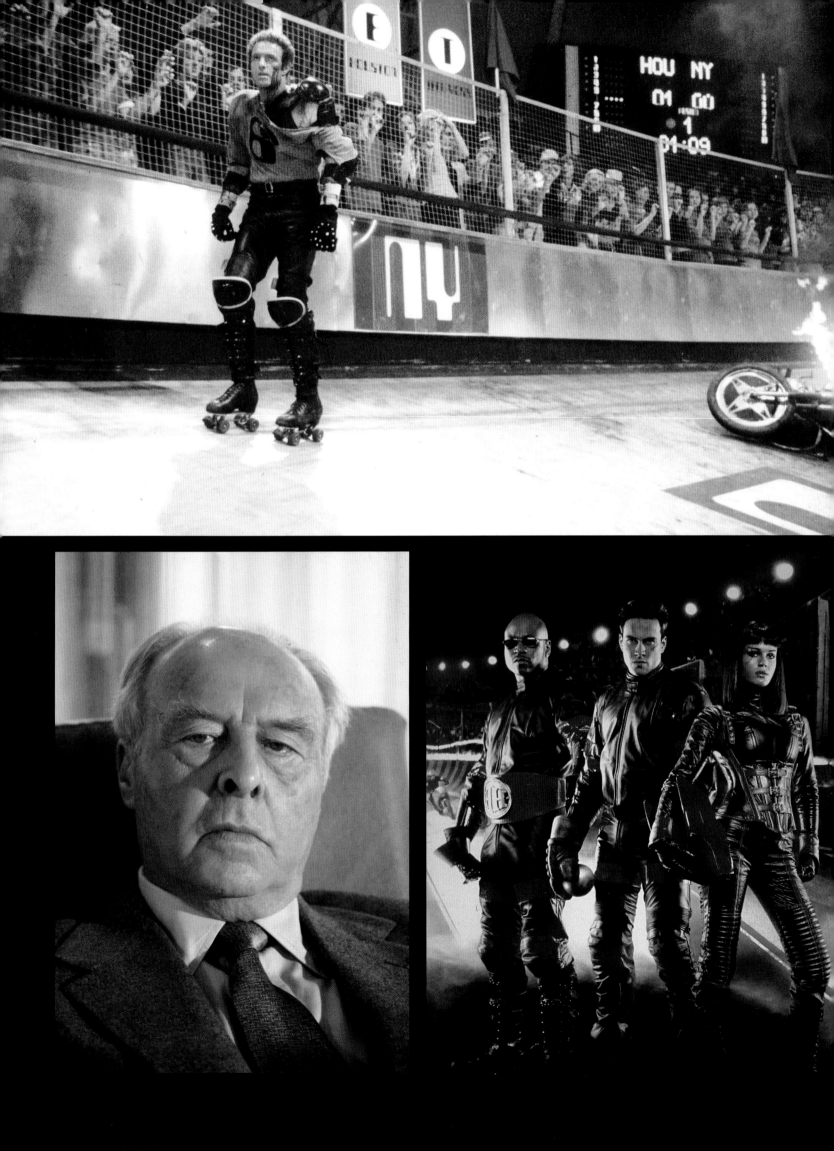

claiming that children should be able to see the cautionary tale despite the violence. Jewison felt the film's message was being misinterpreted as violence for violence's sake. Despite the ratings controversy, *Rollerball* was a box office success—and as proof that Jewison's vision has started to catch up with reality, when the film was remade in 2002, it was set in the present day.

### Logan's Run
*"Don't go in there! You don't have to die! No one has to die at thirty!"*

The twenty-third-century world of *Logan's Run* (1976) is not a dystopian wasteland. It is, rather, a utopia . . . or so it seems. Civilization exists entirely inside a large, domed city operated by a super computer. Every need and desire—mostly desire—is catered to by the computer, and everyday life is idyllic. While sex is offered freely, the computer handles human reproduction. There's only one small catch: what the computer giveth, it also taketh away, and any person who reaches thirty years of age is notified by the crystal embedded into their palm that it is time to be "reborn" in a ritual performed at a location containing the massive "Carousel." What is promised as rebirth, however, is really death.

Those who try to escape their fate and flee are pursued by officers called Sandmen, who are charged with bringing them back. One Sandman, Logan 5 (Michael York), stumbles across a kind of underground railroad for runners that leads outside the dome to Sanctuary. Logan is instructed by the computer to destroy Sanctuary and is activated for Carousel vaporization early, so as to be convincing. With the help of a young woman who is part of the underground, Jessica (Jenny Agutter), Logan becomes a genuine runner and discovers that a ruined world exists outside the dome and that old people still do exist. He returns to the dome to argue against the lie of the Carousel and is interrogated by the computer, which he shorts out by saying that there is no Sanctuary, only a world outside the dome. The dome breaks down, allowing other people to leave and discover the outer world.

Based on the novel by William F. Nolan and George Clayton Johnson (though the original cut-off age was twenty-one, not thirty), *Logan's Run* depicted a highly futuristic environment, much of which, ironically, actually existed. Many scenes were shot on location in Texas; the modernistic Hyatt Regency in Houston, the Water Gardens in Fort Worth, and the Great Hall at the Market Center in Dallas stood in for twenty-third-century buildings. Other settings, such as the Carousel, the ice cavern guarded by a strange robot named Box, were built full-size on MGM soundstages. Given its bright, clean, colorful settings and traditional special effects (which would win a Special Achievement Oscar, because no Best Visual Effects category existed in 1976), *Logan's Run* is one of the last "old-style" sci-fi movies Hollywood produced. Its primary innovation was the use of holography. During Logan's interrogation his mind is fragmented into six pieces, all of which display behind him.

A short-lived television series based on the film premiered on CBS in 1977.

***Above***: *Jenny Agutter and Michael York learn about the unknown world outside the dome from Peter Ustinov in Logan's Run.*

***Opposite top***: *Logan 5 (Michael York) is persuaded by rebel Jessica (Jenny Agutter) that things are not as they seem in the futuristic Logan's Run.*

***Opposite bottom***: *The "Carousel" of Logan's Run where people go for "rebirth," never to return.*

*Above*: Inside the domed city of Logan's Run.

*Right*: Logan (Michael York) and Jessica (Jenny Agutter) discover the world beyond the Dome is far less perfect in Logan's Run.

*Left*: Logan (Michael York) and Jessica (Jenny Agutter) enter a cold and dangerous would-be escape route ruled by the robot "Box" (Roscoe Lee Browne, somewhere inside the casing).

*Below*: After returning to the Dome, Logan (Michael York) undergoes interrogation in Logan's Run.

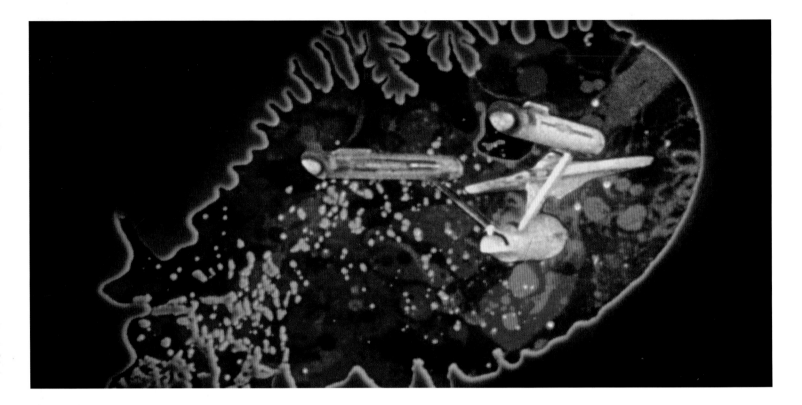

# "Space . . . the final frontier."

Had Lucille Ball not believed that television had fallen into a formulaic rut in the mid-1960s, the sci-fi universe might be *very* different today.

What does the wacky redhead have to do with any of it? Just that Lucy, in addition to being one of television's top stars of the time, was also one of the medium's savviest producers. "The public deserves more creativity from TV," Ball stated in 1965, right after the production company she ran, Desilu Productions, financed the first pilot for a revolutionary new series called *Star Trek*.

*Star Trek*, which premiered on NBC in 1966, was the brainchild of former-LAPD-officer-turned-television-writer Gene Roddenberry. It focused on the mission of the USS *Enterprise*, which was to explore new worlds and life forms on behalf of the United Federation of Planets, and "boldly go where no man had gone before." During its exploration, the crew also tries to stop the aggression of such alien races as the Klingons and the Romulans.

To foster the federation concept, the regular crew was something of an interplanetary United Nations. Lieutenant Uhura, played by Nichelle Nichols, was an African American woman, and strange as it may seem today, casting a black actress in such a prominent, authoritative role was a daring move. Even Dr. Martin Luther King Jr., was a fan of Nichols. Chief Engineer Montgomery Scott, played by James Doohan, was a Scotsman (though Doohan was really Canadian). There was also a Russian (Ensign Chekov, played by Walter Koenig), a Japanese American (helmsman Sulu; George Takei) and a half-Vulcan, half-Human (science officer Spock; Leonard Nimoy). In charge of the *Enterprise* was the steady Captain James Tiberius Kirk, in the show an Iowa native but played by Canadian William Shatner, a former Shakespearean actor who had been working his way up the Hollywood ranks since the late 1950s. (In the show's first, rejected pilot, 1950s heartthrob Jeffrey Hunter played Captain Christopher Pike.)

Of the crew, it was Spock—the only character carried over from the initial pilot—who became the breakout character, serving as the sometimes maddeningly logical voice of reason, often as counterpoint to grouchy Dr. Leonard McCoy (DeForrest Kelley), who wore his emotions on his sleeve.

What was most immediately noticeable about *Star Trek* was its physical look: the

**Above**: *James Doohan, DeForest Kelley, Walter Koenig, Majel Barrett, William Shatner, Nichelle Nichols, Leonard Nimoy, and George Takei report to the bridge on* Star Trek.

**Opposite**: *While somewhat rudimentary when seen today, the special effects for the original* Star Trek *were eye-popping at the time—particularly for television.*

atmospheric cinematography and special effects, courtesy of a large effects team led by James Rugg, Howard A. Anderson, and Linwood Dunn, were beyond anything else on the tube at that time. The effects not only included the model work but also the show's signature transporter technology, or "beaming." Beaming consisted of combining such tried-and-true film techniques as traveling mattes—optically compositing two different images into the same shot—with dissolves, the gradual fading of one shot into another. The signature look of beaming up—the moving particle imagery—was created by filming aluminum dust shot through a beam of light. Audiences may have come to *Star Trek* for the effects, futuristic sets, and colorful alien characters, but they stayed for the stories and the human element. One of *Star Trek*'s most famous innovations had nothing to do with sci-fi: the 1968 episode "Plato's Stepchildren" featured TV's first interracial kiss, between Shatner and Nichols.

Despite its impact on sci-fi, *Star Trek* battled for ratings. By the third season, budgets had been cut by 10 percent and NBC's already tenuous support of the show was fading. A letter-writing campaign (basically the first of its kind) had saved the show from cancellation after its first season, but in 1969, to the outrage of fans, the show was finally canceled. However, it was anything but dead. In fact, its resurrection would achieve epic proportions.

While the cast (except for Koenig) reassembled for an animated *Star Trek* series in 1973, the franchise's real second act began in 1979 with the release of *Star Trek: The Motion Picture*, directed by Robert Wise. The crew was all a little older, a little grayer, a tad heavier, but ready for the mission nonetheless. Five more sequels featuring the entire main original cast followed (including *Star Trek II: The Wrath of Khan*, in which Spock famously died . . . but not for long), before ending with *Star Trek VI: The Undiscovered Country* in 1991. By

**Top**: Leonard Nimoy as Spock and Jeffrey Hunter as Captain Pike in the original pilot film for Star Trek. Clips from the pilot were recycled into the two-part episode "The Menagerie."

**Above left**: The new crew of the Enterprise for Star Trek: The Next Generation: (front) Brent Spiner, Jonathan Frakes, Patrick Stewart, LeVar Burton; (rear) Wil Wheaton, Marina Sirtis, Michael Dorn, Gates McFadden, and Whoopi Goldberg.

**Above right**: The cast of Star Trek: Deep Space Nine: (front) Armin Shimerman, Rene Auberjonois, Avery Brooks, Nana Visitor, Colm Meaney; (rear) Michael Dorn, Terry Farrell, Cirroc Lofton.

**Above**: "Beam me up" has become part of our lexicon.

**Right**: Star Trek: Voyager featured the first female captain, in the form of Kate Mulgrew (center), seen here with Robert Beltran, Robert Duncan McNeill, and Robert Picardo.

then, though, a new mission had taken over television: *Star Trek: The Next Generation* (1987–94), which was set aboard a new starship *Enterprise*, with a new captain, Jean-Luc Picard (Patrick Stewart). In the intervening years between the time settings of the two series, The Klingons had become allies of the Federation, though there was still no shortage of antagonistic cultures in the universe. *Star Trek: The Next Generation* aired in syndication, and in 1994 made history as the first syndicated program ever nominated for an Emmy for Best Dramatic Series.

A feature-film spin-off, *Star Trek Generations* was released in 1994, featuring both the new *Enterprise* crew and many of the original crew in a story that contrived for them to meet. *Star Trek: First*

*Contact* (1996), *Star Trek: Insurrection* (1998), and *Star Trek: Nemesis* (2002) followed in theaters. Meanwhile, on television, *Star Trek: Deep Space Nine*, something of a departure in that it was set aboard a space station, premiered in syndication in 1993 and enjoyed a seven-season run. *Star Trek: Voyager*, set on the starship *Voyager*, also enjoyed a seven-season run. *Voyager* broke new ground in the world of *Star Trek* by featuring a female captain, Kathryn Janeway (Kate Mulgrew). Significantly, by this time the *Star Trek* franchise was so powerful that Paramount—the owner of *Star Trek* after Lucille Ball sold Desilu to the studio in the 1960s—used *Voyager* as the anchor series that launched its new television network, UPN, in 1995. The fourth spin-off series, *Star Trek: Enterprise*, premiered in 2001 on UPN and ran for four seasons.

**Above**: *Director J. J. Abrams and cast on the* Enterprise *set of the 2009 reboot of* Star Trek.

**Opposite**: *Scott Bakula and Jolene Blaylock (left) encounter a Blue Man Group of a different sort in television's* Star Trek: Enterprise.

For a show that had wobbly ratings in its original run, *Star Trek* has become one of the most popular, lucrative, and spun-off properties in history. Merchandising for the franchise alone is more profitable than all revenue for most television shows or movies. Conventions, websites, novelizations, video games, fan fiction, and other spin-offs abound. *Star Trek* has truly become part of pop culture and references to it are too numerous to list, though one of the most notable and affectionate remains the 1999 comedy movie, *Galaxy Quest*, which is about the stars of an old sci-fi series who find themselves actually having to save the universe.

Everything came full cycle in 2009 with a major big-screen reboot, *Star Trek*, directed by J. J. Abrams, featuring an entirely new cast playing the original crew. Well, *almost* an entirely new cast: the script managed to carve out a cameo for Leonard Nimoy as "Spock Prime," allowing him to go boldly where he'd gone so many times before.

Today, such lines as "Beam me up, Scotty," and "I'm a doctor, Jim, not a [fill in the blank]," inaccurately quoted though they are, have entered our lexicon and become part of our culture. It would appear that for the foreseeable future at least, we're all going to keep on Trekkin'.

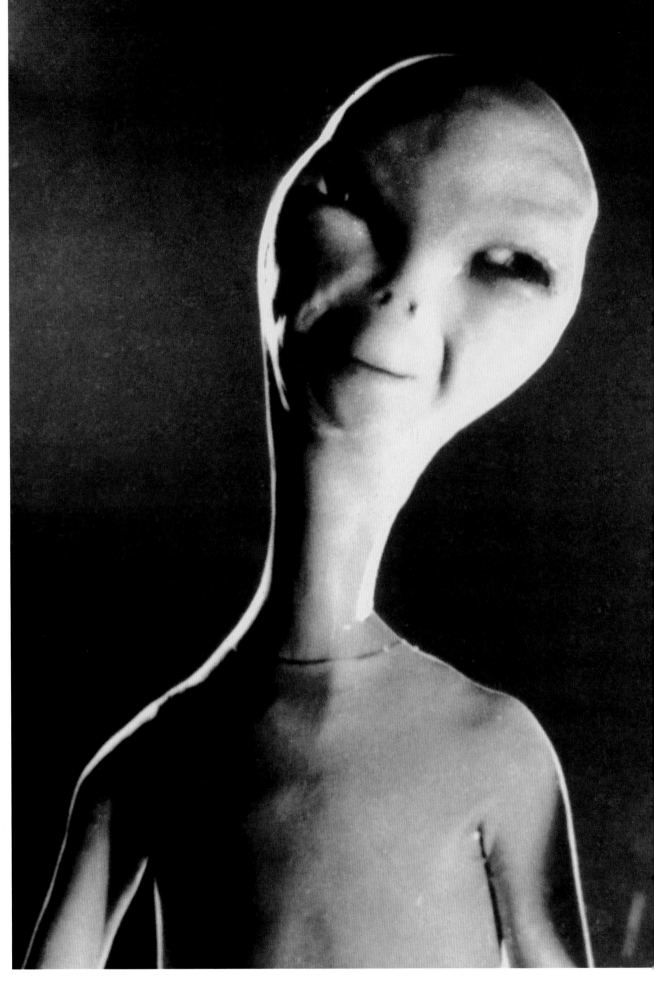

# A NEW
# BEGINNING

# 06

The 1970s saw not simply a renaissance of the science fiction film but a virtual reinvention of it. It wasn't just that the look and feel of the genre received a major makeover—though it did, through the development of computer-controlled special effects pioneered by George Lucas's Industrial Light and Magic. It wasn't just that it sounded different—though it did, through a combination of innovative sound-effects work by the likes of Walter Murch and the portentous, neoclassical musical scores of John Williams, which supplanted the "mod" electronic scores of a few years earlier. It was that Hollywood itself changed during this period, both in the way films were made and the way they were marketed. A new concept was born—the planned trilogy—and merchandizing would become as vital a part of the filmmaking industry as scriptwriting.

The reason for these changes can be summed up in five words: George Lucas and Steven Spielberg. There were, of course, others involved, but it would be these two, whether working individually or together, who spearheaded the new beginning of sci-fi.

### Close Encounters of the Third Kind
#### *"Da-de-da-duh-daaaaa..."*

The science fiction films of the 1950s, on which Steven Spielberg had been raised, were often couched as warnings, presenting alien forces that were outright threats to the people of Earth. Spielberg's vision of interplanetary contact two decades later was entirely different: it was wondrous and nonthreatening, even childlike. This was exemplified by the director's *Close Encounters of the Third Kind* (1977), the title referring to the classification of UFO/alien sighting that involves actually seeing an "animate being."

The message of *Close Encounters* is simple: the aliens come, they see, they don't conquer. Average people such as Roy Neary (Richard Dreyfuss), a power lineman, find themselves encountering UFOs and receiving mysterious mental messages that correspond to a mountainous shape. Like others, Roy becomes obsessed with the thought of flying saucers, so much so that his alarmed wife leaves him. After seeing a television report about a train derailment by the monumental Devil's Tower in Wyoming, Roy realizes that he is not insane; Devil's Tower is the mental image haunting him. Drawn there, he discovers a secret government base has been established to make contact with the aliens. An enormous glowing spaceship arrives at the base, communicating with a simple five-note musical motif with the UFO researchers, led by Claude Lacomb (François Truffaut). The government forces decide that some earthlings may accompany the aliens back to their home planet, and Roy is among them. The aliens emerge from the ship to welcome them aboard.

The seed for *Close Encounters* was an 8mm sci-fi epic called *Firelight* that Spielberg made when he was sixteen years old. Twenty-nine-year-old Spielberg's casting of François Truffaut in a key role in *Close Encounters* surprised some in Hollywood. Not only was this Truffaut's only English-language film as an actor (his English had improved since directing *Fahrenheit 451*), it was his only performance in a film he did not direct himself. And John Williams's five-note theme, used in the film as a means of contact between Earth scientists and the aliens, became quite possibly the world's shortest hit song.

**Above**: *The "mother ship" comes down over Devil's Tower in* Close Encounters of the Third Kind.

**Opposite**: *One of effects artist Carlo Rambaldi's animatronic aliens in* Close Encounters of the Third Kind.

*Right: Steven Spielberg on the set of* Close Encounters of the Third Kind.

*Below: Children in alien costumes were used for group shots of the extra-terrestrials in* Close Encounters of the Third Kind.

*Opposite top: Lineman Roy Neary (Richard Dreyfuss) has a title experience in* Close Encounters of the Third Kind.

*Opposite bottom: Melinda Dillon and Cary Guffey fear what they can't see in* Close Encounters of the Third Kind.

The primary alien seen at the end of the picture was a humanoid animatronic puppet designed by Carlo Rambaldi, who in the 1970s had cornered the market in this particular form of special effects, having created the forty-foot ape figure and limb components for the 1976 remake of *King Kong*. His work was so effective that several years before *Close Encounters* he had to go into an Italian court to prove that images of extreme abuse to animals in the Italian film *A Lizard in a Woman's Skin* (1971) did not show actual abuse but was the result of his special effects creations. Rambaldi's testimony prevented the film's director, Lucio Fulci, from serving a jail term! More than two decades later, J. J. Abrams paid homage to Carlo Rambaldi in his hit ABC sci-fi series *Alias*, by naming a mysterious and prophetic character who was technologically centuries ahead of his time "Milo Giacomo Rambaldi."

Unlike the sleek, seamless spaceships of past films, the alien mother ship had a highly detailed surface that resembled a futuristic building from an early expressionistic sci-fi film. It contained a potent in-joke as well, courtesy of Dennis Muren, a key special-effects artist at George Lucas's Industrial Light and Magic. Having just worked on *Star Wars*, Muren put a small model of R2-D2 on the stern of the spaceship.

*Above*: A menacing Cylon from TV's Battlestar Galactica.

*Right*: Dirk Benedict, Richard Hatch, Lorne Greene, and Maren Jensen from the original 1978 series Battlestar Galactica.

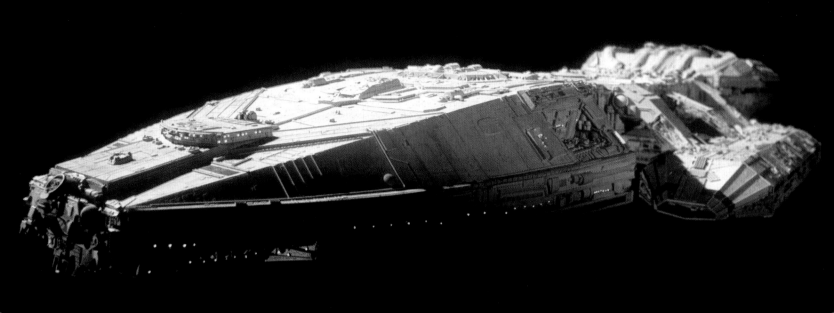

### Battlestar Galactica

*"There are those who believe that life here began out there."*

Little within the television industry is released without hype, and the hype for *Battlestar Galactica*, which premiered on ABC the fall of 1978, was that it was the most expensive weekly television series ever made, costing upwards of a million dollars per episode. Created by the prolific TV producer Glen A. Larson, the show featured the adventures of the crew of *Galactica*, the last remaining warship, or "battlestar," that had been fighting a menacing robotic race called Cylons for a thousand years. (It's not that the Cylons are evil by nature so much as they were never given a cease-fire order by their creators.) Commander Adama (Lorne Green), who helms the *Galactica*, is also responsible for a "ragtag" fleet of smaller craft, all of which are trying to escape further conflict by seeking out a faraway, inhabitable planet called . . . Earth. The premise of the series further implies that Adama's Earth-like race was descended from one of twelve colony planets (read tribes) of star travelers who came to Earth in millennia past and influenced what would become the civilizations of the Mayans, the Toltecs, and the ancient Egyptians. The quasi-religious/mythological thread, mixed with the pseudo-scientific "ancient astronauts" theory that was popular at the time, was reflected in many of the characters' names: Adama, Apollo, Sheba, Athena, and Cassiopeia among them. In fact, the original title of the series was to be *Adama's Ark*.

No one at the time questioned that *Battlestar Galactica* was produced in the wake of the success of *Star Wars*, though there were some who felt the connection went far beyond jumping onto a popular bandwagon. 20th Century Fox, the studio behind *Star Wars*, actually filed a plagiarism suit against the series. Universal Television, which produced *Battlestar Galactica*, countersued, claiming that *Star Wars* had stolen from Universal properties all the way back to the 1930s *Buck Rogers* serial! Caught somewhere in the middle was special-effects artist John Dykstra, who developed the series's miniature effects and had just won an Oscar for *Star Wars*.

*Battlestar Galactica* lasted only one season under that name then came back as a midseason, lower-budgeted, and short-lived show titled *Galactica 1980*. In 2004, the property had one of the most successful revivals in television history when Syfy unveiled its new *Battlestar Galactica*, starring Edward James Olmos as Commander Adama. This reboot was much more serious minded, though it had just as many religious and mystical allusions as the original. It was also more immediately successful and won a prestigious Peabody Award. The new *Battlestar Galactica* spawned a string of television movies and spin-offs, including the Syfy series *Caprica* (2010).

The new Battlestar Galactica ("BSG" to fans) was heavily influenced by the concerns of a post-9/11 world. In many ways, BSG transcended being just an entertainment property: as evidenced by the fact that in March of 2009, the United Nations hosted a panel discussion featuring key BSG writer-producers and cast members. Also on the panel were a handful of UN commissioners in areas such as human rights, policy planning, and a special representative for "Children and Armed Conflict." New York City public school students were invited to attend this discussion held in one of the UN's large, semi-circular conference rooms. Topics discussed included human rights, terrorism, the plight of children during wartime, and the intersection between religious faith and politics. It was quite the heady and important evening!

*Above*: Battlestar Galactica's *special effects were reminiscent of those in* Star Wars *. . . a little too reminiscent for 20th Century Fox, which filed suit.*

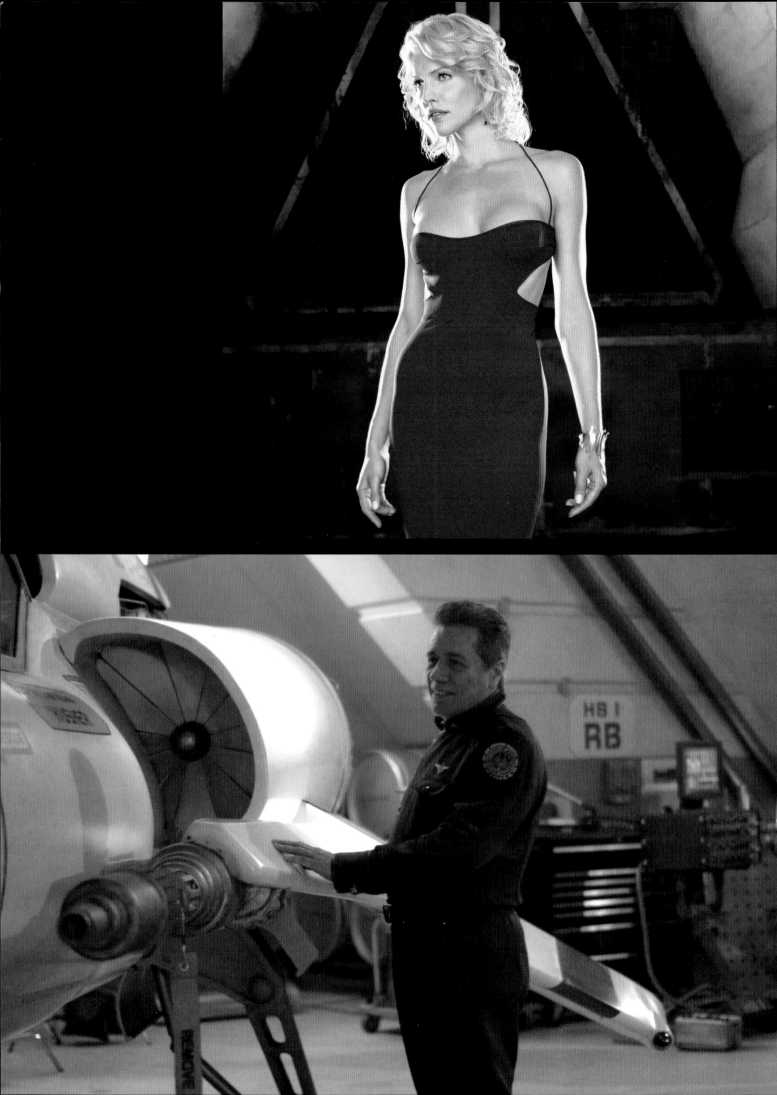

### Alien

#### "In space no one can hear you scream."

Director Ridley Scott's *Alien* (1979) established the prototype for the modern melding of sci-fi film and horror movie. It is widely heralded for two things: the scene where the parasitic alien life form that has inadvertently been brought on board the spaceship *Nostromo* suddenly bursts through the chest of crewman Kane (John Hurt), and escapes; and the fact that its principal protagonist, Ripley (Sigourney Weaver), is not a weak, fluttery heroine who needs to be saved but a woman who kicks some serious alien and android butt. (She does like cats, though.) Screenwriter Dan O'Bannon had originally envisioned all the roles as male; the producers, David Giler and Walter Hill, were the ones who decided to cast a woman. The role of the resourceful survivor of the alien's predatory hunt made Weaver a star.

Filming the film's signature "chest-burster" scene was every bit as shocking and gross for the other actors—Weaver, Veronica Cartwright, Ian Holm, Yaphet Kotto, Harry Dean Stanton, and Tom Skerritt—as it was for the audience. Hurt's head and arms were real, but the rest of him was concealed under a table while the false chest through which the "chest-burster" alien puppet would emerge was on top. The cast knew that a puppet was going to burst forth, but they were not expecting its force, nor the blood and actual animal offal that accompanied it. The shock and disgust actress Cartwright shows on camera after being doused in blood was genuine. This scene would be re-created by Mel Brooks, of all people, in his 1987 spoof *Spaceballs*, for which he convinced John Hurt to replay the role of Kane in a surprise cameo.

The fully grown creature was designed by artist H. R. Giger, and its articulated head was built by Carlo Rambaldi; the latex body suit was custom-built to fit the seven-foot-two-inch, very thin Bolaji Badejo, a Nigerian design student whom Scott had met in a bar. A series of models in varying sizes were made to represent the *Nostromo* (named after Joseph Conrad's novel about a South African mining town), with the exterior details coming from bits and pieces cannibalized from commercial plastic model kits. The organic body parts, human and alien, seen throughout the film were not fabricated. To depict flesh and guts, the special-effects team sometimes used animal parts and other times went to the grocery store for pasta, oysters, caviar, and onion rings, all of which were utilized to gooey, gross effect.

*Alien* was an enormous hit, and Weaver returned for the rematch in director James Cameron's *Aliens* (1986), which earned Weaver a Best Actress Academy Award nomination. *Alien 3* followed in 1992 and featured Ripley's death, and *Alien Resurrection*, featuring Weaver as a part-human, part-alien clone of the original Ripley, in 1997. No incarnation of Ripley was seen in 2004's *Alien vs. Predator*, a combination of two popular franchises that was based on a comic book teaming, or its follow-up, *Alien vs. Predator: Requiem* (2007).

*Above*: Sigourney Weaver and director Ridley Scott on the set of *Alien*.

*Opposite top*: How the Cylons have changed! Tricia Helfer as Cylon Number Six in TV's rebooted Battlestar Galactica *(2004)*.

*Opposite bottom*: Edward James Olmos as Captain Adama in the 2004 television reworking of Battlestar Galactica.

**Above**: John Hurt takes ill at dinner and prompts the most famous scene from Alien.

**Left**: The "chest-buster" from Alien; even most of the cast did not know what was going to happen until the cameras were running.

*Right*: The alien from Alien.

*Below*: Ripley (Sigourney Weaver) gets some unwanted face time with the creature in Alien 3 (1992).

**Top**: A cloned Ripley (Sigourney Weaver, center) isn't messing around in Alien Resurrection (1997), with Ron Perlman and Winona Ryder.

**Above**: As designed by artist H. R. Giger, the Alien has become one of the most iconic creatures of the postwar twentieth century.

**Left**: Ripley (Sigourney Weaver) and the child Newt (Carrie Henn) confront the Alien Queen in Aliens (1986).

### Mad Max

**"And the Road Warrior . . . he lives now, only in my memories."**

It is rare that a film sequel tops the original in all ways. *Mad Max 2: The Road Warrior* (1981), the follow-up to *Mad Max* (1979), is one of the greatest examples of that rarity.

The original, a low-budget, high-octane chase film about a near-future policeman turned vigilante, was made in Australia by a first-time filmmaker, George Miller, and starred then-unknown Mel Gibson. (Miller, incidentally, has frequently been confused with a contemporary Australian filmmaker, also named George Miller, who directed the 1982 film *The Man From Snowy River*, but they are different men.) Essentially a chase-and-car-crash film shot on the highways outside Melbourne, *Mad Max* received mixed critical reaction in the United States, with many critics objecting to the poor voice dubbing that had replaced the original Aussie "Strine" dialect with flat American accents. It did, however, gain a cult following. More importantly, it was the first independent film to capitalize on Hollywood's new fascination with trilogies.

*Mad Max 2: The Road Warrior* was co-written and directed by George Miller and again starred Mel Gibson as "Mad" Max Rockatansky. However, Gibson's star had risen considerably in the intervening two years. *Mad Max 2* added a mythical level to the chase; with Miller-cited inspiration from both samurai films and the writings of Joseph Campbell (sources that also inspired *Star Wars*). The film is set further into the future, during a time when nuclear conflicts between two warrior tribes have rendered the world (or at least Australia) a wasteland, and when the most precious commodity on the planet is gasoline. Max is now a drifter and a scavenger, taking what food and gasoline he can from wrecked vehicles—or those whose crashes he facilitates. Happening upon a sort of range war between a group of settlers living near an oil refinery and the menacing marauders and bike warriors, Max fights on the side of the settlers. He also befriends a boy known as the "Feral Kid," who communicates nonverbally. After defeating the marauders in explosive fashion, enabling the settlers to escape with precious fuel to start a new tribe, Max continues on his lonely way. At the close of the film it is revealed that the story was related from the memory of the Feral Kid, who is now the elder of the tribe.

*Above*: Mel Gibson looks barely out of high school in Mad Max *(1979). It would take the sequel,* Mad Max 2: The Road Warrior *to make him a superstar.*

**Top**: *Vernon Wells as the brutal Wez in* Mad Max 2:
The Road Warrior.

**Above left**: *Max has put in a few more miles by the
time of* Mad Max 2: The Road Warrior *(1981).*

**Above right**: *The action chase scenes in* Mad Max
2: The Road Warrior *helped it become a huge critical as well as commercial hit.*

Unlike the reception for *Mad Max*, which was dismissed as a cheap B movie, this time most critics fell over themselves praising *Mad Max 2: The Road Warrior*, particularly for its action and stunt work. (A more cynical view is that its dialogue was not dubbed this time, thereby categorizing it as a foreign film, and American film critics *love* foreign films.) The sequel was touted as the most expensive and complex Australian film to date, its budget more than ten times that of *Mad Max*. The third chapter in the trilogy, *Mad Max: Beyond Thunderdome*, released in 1985, had major studio backing, and was targeted to a larger, more mainstream audience. Miller concentrated solely on the action scenes and passed the dialogue sequences to co-director George Ogilvie. The film featured Tina Turner, then at the peak of her stardom, in the role of the antagonist, Aunty Entity, who is in charge of an outpost called Bartertown, which is powered by a methane factory. The Thunderdome in question is a gladiatorial-style arena where combatants resolve conflicts to the death. At the end, Max's story seems to be forming into a mythology, as it is told many years later by a former child he helped rescue. *Mad Max: Beyond Thunderdome* was also that rare sci-fi film to spawn a hit song, Turner's "We Don't Need Another Hero (Thunderdome)."

*Top: Rock diva Tina Turner was an offbeat choice for the antagonist role in* Mad Max: Beyond Thunderdome *(1985).*

***Above:*** *Jaw-dropping car stunts, like this one from* Mad Max: Beyond Thunderdome, *done without special effects, characterize the entire* Mad Max *franchise.*

### E.T. the Extra-Terrestrial
### *"E.T. phone home."*

If the aliens of *Close Encounters of the Third Kind* were friendly, the wide-eyed, puppyish, Reese's Pieces–munching star of Steven Spielberg's *E.T. the Extra-Terrestrial* (1982) was the cuddliest and most lovable ever seen in any galaxy. The director once more employed his uniquely childlike vision to tell the story of the discovery of a space alien who has been separated from his fellow travelers and stranded on Earth. This time the story is told from the point of view of real children: a lonely, fatherless, ten-year-old boy named Elliot (Henry Thomas), his five-year-old sister, Gertie (Drew Barrymore), and his taunting older brother, Michael (Robert MacNaughton). The adults in the film are represented by the kids' preoccupied mom, Mary (Dee Wallace), and the sinister governmental figures tracking the remaining alien, led by the ambiguous, unnamed agent known as "Keys" (because of the ring of keys he wears), played by Peter Coyote. For many of the scenes that involved both the kids and grown-ups,

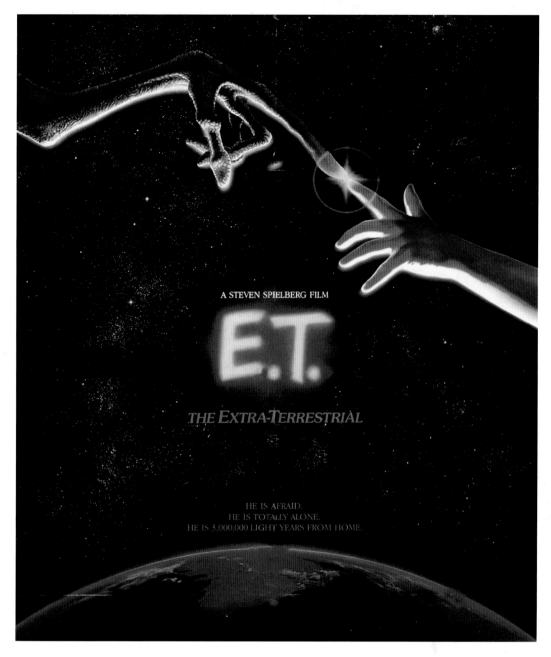

Spielberg employed low camera angles to replicate a child's visual point of view.

The real star of the film, however, was E.T. himself. Carlo Rambaldi designed the animatronic version of E.T. used for close-ups and key acting scenes. For other shots, the character was played by a little person in a less expressive costume. The combination of these two techniques resulted in a character that proved to be the most convincingly real and affecting artificial being since Disney's Pinocchio. *E.T.* was a huge, influential hit that created a national catchphrase, "E.T. phone home," inspired a hit song for Neil Diamond called "Heartlight" (in the film, E.T.'s heart glows red), and provided Spielberg's Amblin Entertainment with its company logo: Elliott and E.T. bicycling past the full moon.

Despite the film's success, though, Spielberg had not been 100 percent satisfied with some of the shots. One scene involving E.T. in a bathtub was cut from the film because the performance of Rambaldi's creation wasn't up to par. "When you're working with an animatronics character like that, day in and day out, you have your good days and your bad days, and that was a bad day," remembered producer Kathleen Kennedy. "We couldn't get E.T. to perform quite the way Steven wanted him to do in the sequence. Sometimes you have to abandon an original idea and move on." In preparation for the film's twentieth anniversary, however, Spielberg and Kennedy went back and spruced up some of the special-effects shots with digital technology, putting the newly animated bathtub scene back in for the 2002 re-release. One deleted scene that did not make it back into the re-release involved Elliott being chewed out by the headmaster of his school, played by Harrison Ford. Oh, and those Reese's Pieces? They were a last minute substitution for M&M's, which Spielberg originally wanted to use but could not get the rights for from . . . wait for it . . . the *Mars* candy company.

*Above*: The image of E.T.'s glowing finger touching Elliot's human one is almost as famous as the Michelangelo fresco painting that inspired it.

*Opposite top*: This iconic shot of Elliot and E.T. cycling past the moon became the company logo for Steven Spielberg's Amblin Entertainment.

*Opposite bottom*: E.T. (here a small actor in a suit) prepares to go home in E.T. the Extra-Terrestrial.

**Top**: *Drew Barrymore became a star as a result of E.T. the Extra-Terrestrial.*

**Above**: *Elliot (Henry Thomas), Gertie (Drew Barrymore), and Michael (Robert MacNaughton) investigate their strange visitor in E.T. the Extra-Terrestrial.*

**Opposite**: *Carlo Rambaldi's animatronic E.T. figure was capable of a full range of expressions and emotions.*

## Blade Runner
### *"'More than human' is our motto."*

*Top: The noirpunk world of* Blade Runner.

*Above: Harrison Ford's Rick Deckard was no fashion plate in* Blade Runner.

Based on Philip K. Dick's novel *Do Androids Dream of Electric Sheep?* and directed by Ridley Scott, 1982's *Blade Runner* is a seminal example of noirpunk: even though it is set in the Los Angeles of 2019 and features all the flying vehicles, Jumbotron screens, and robotics that people thirty years ago envisioned would be here by now, its dark, smoky, shadowy atmosphere—even its hair and costume designs—are pure film noir. The only thing it lacked was the image of star Harrison Ford in a fedora—how ironic is that?

Rick Deckard (Ford) is a former "blade runner," a police officer whose job is to track down and "retire" (read kill) escaped replicants, the highly sophisticated, highly realistic synthetic people built by the shadowy Tyrell Corporation that are used for service or pleasure (sex) work on Earth's outer-terrestrial colonies. Replicants have been banned on Earth, but a group of them have commandeered a spaceship and have returned. Deckard is coerced by his former supervisor into taking the job of hunting the fugitive robots down. During the course of his travels down the futuristic mean streets, he encounters the beautiful Rachael (Sean Young), a replicant who doesn't know she's a replicant. The details of what happens beyond that rough synopsis depends on which version of *Blade Runner* one is watching; there are three primary versions of the film, but a total of *seven* different iterations have been shown publicly.

Industrial designer Syd Mead was hired to consult on the look of *Blade Runner* (which Ridley Scott described as "an adult comic strip"). The decision was made that nothing would look shiny and new. Rather, the premise fueling the design was that in the Los Angeles of the twenty-first century, it is too expensive to demolish old buildings and replace them with new ones, so the property owners simply fix them up as best they can, resulting in patchwork cityscapes with all the seams and cracks still visible. New York Street on the Warner Bros. back lot in Burbank was revamped for the movie's downtown area, and other scenes were shot inside L.A.'s historic Bradbury Building, a Victorian-era wrought-iron-and-glass masterpiece that is the physical embodiment of steampunk. The building's designer, George Wyman, cited as an influence Edward Bellamy's 1887 sci-fi novel *Looking Backward*, which is set in the year 2000. (And while the Bradbury Building has no connection to Ray Bradbury, Wyman's grandson, Forrest J Ackerman, was the man most widely credited for coining the term "sci-fi.")

Upon its initial release *Blade Runner* confused critics and performed disappointingly at the box office, but has since become a cult icon . . . in all of its versions.

**Top**: *Zhora (Joanna Cassidy) is "retired" by Deckard in* Blade Runner.

**Above**: *Daryl Hannah as Pris in* Blade Runner.

*Above*: The future goes retro: Sean Young in Blade Runner.

***Below***: *Harrison Ford as Deckard, in a scene from* Blade Runner *shot in L.A.'s Victorian-era futuristic Bradbury Building.*

**Above**: *The early days of computer-generated scenery, from* Tron.

### Tron

*"On the other side of the screen, it all looks so easy."*

For years the Walt Disney Studios had a sideline that few really thought about: special effects. Not only did the studio break new ground for its own pictures, such as *Mary Poppins* (1964) and even *The Love Bug* (1969), but it was the go-to company if anyone else in Hollywood needed tricky special effects. Optical effects for both *Forbidden Planet* (1956) and *The Birds* (1963) were handled by Disney technicians on loan-out. In 1982, Disney updated its effects résumé on home turf with *Tron*, the first film to extensively use computer imagery. The fact that the look of the film is far less eye-popping today than it was thirty years ago is less an indictment of *Tron* than a demonstration of how far digital imagery has advanced (or, to put it another way, just compare a film made in 1909 with *Gone with the Wind*).

*Tron* stars Jeff Bridges as Kevin Flynn, a genius computer programmer for a company called ENCOM. He hacks into the company mainframe to obtain proof that his boss, Dillinger (David Warner), has stolen his work—only he is physically drawn inside the computer by its Master Control Program (MCP). Once "inside," he is ordered to compete in games against a computerized version of Dillinger called Sark. Aiding him is Tron (Bruce Boxleitner), the digital embodiment of a security program developed by a co-worker of Flynn named Bradley (also Boxleitner). MCP, an incarnation of Dillinger, is in charge of the games, which become more and more dangerous, but Flynn manages to defeat the computer brain and return to the outside world with the evidence he needs.

Disney veteran Harrison Ellenshaw and Richard Taylor supervised the special effects for *Tron*, for which Syd Mead, Jean "Moebius" Giraud, and Peter Lloyd were artistic consultants. However it was not an entirely digital shoot. Sequences set on the "Grid" were computer generated, but most of the action was traditionally filmed in black and white on sets

*Above*: Jeff Bridges as Flynn, while still in control of the machines, in Tron.

*Opposite top*: David Warner as the command program Sark in Tron.

*Opposite bottom*: Cindy Mogan as Yori and Bruce Boxleitner as Tron wear matching digital costumes—not to mention expressions—in Tron.

draped with black duvetyne to block out any detail. The backgrounds were added digitally and the characters were colored via rotoscoping, an old animation technique of drawing or painting over frames of footage. *Tron* was denied consideration for a Best Visual Effects Oscar that year because the Academy felt digital imagery was not eligible as an effect. How times have changed.

Bridges, Boxleitner, and Warner were reunited for 2010's *Tron: Legacy*, which pointed out in boldface the advancements in the digital effects realm since the original, including the use of digital 3-D. In this sequel, Flynn's son Sam (Garrett Hedlund) is running ENCOM. He receives a mysterious message from his father, who had disappeared over twenty years before. Bradley encourages Sam to follow it up. Sam finds the old computer and gets sucked into the Grid, where he locates both his father and his father's program but faces the computer's perilous challenges. One of the most notable effects of *Tron: Legacy* was depicting two different versions of Jeff Bridges, the grizzled, sixty-year-old real one, and a computer-generated younger version that looks as he did in the original movie. Young Flynn was created by having Bridges perform with fifty-two markers on his face and a helmet-mounted camera, which provided information that was then fed into a digital model created from old photos. This time the extensive digital effects were handled by Digital Domain, an effects company founded by James Cameron, Stan Winston, and Scott Ross.

**Top**: *Director Joseph Kosinski (center) speaks with Olivia Wilde and Jeff Bridges on the set of Tron Legacy (2010).*

**Above**: *Tron Legacy: digital effects have improved just a little since the original Tron.*

**Above**: They weren't really our friends, but we
didn't yet know that at the beginning of the
1983 miniseries V.

## V
### "Aw, Mom, he's no E.T."

V (for "Visitors") was a landmark two-part miniseries that premiered on NBC in 1983
and is remembered for its deceptively friendly, human-looking aliens that were actually disguised reptilian horrors who gobble down live birds and guinea pigs when no one is looking.
But what V really represented was a throwback to the kind of cautionary sci-fi that predom-
inated in the 1950s. The aliens look just like us—they wear rubber masks and shield their
lizard eyes—and they claim to have come in peace. Their front person, Diana (Jane Badler),
is outwardly beautiful and reassuring, but before long the Visitors begin to infiltrate power
and usurp control of the planet, under the guise of sharing their advanced technologies. In
particular, they persecute Earth scientists. They also keep the media at bay, especially crusading journalists like Mike Donovan (Marc Singer), who has managed to capture the aliens'
true natures on videotape and realizes that mankind is soon to be on the menu! When the
Visitors take over the media, Donovan becomes a fugitive, eventually joining a rebellion
formed to fight what is now clearly an alien invasion—a task made more difficult by the fact
that the Visitors have managed to line up earthly accomplices to support and protect them.

V—which in the story becomes the tagged symbol of the rebellion—was the most
overtly political sci-fi presentation in decades. An opening sequence held up the guerilla
war that was then occurring in Nicaragua as an example of resistance fighting, and once the
aliens landed, the miniseries was awash with Nazi allusions. In a real throwback to an earlier
time in television, series creator Kenneth Johnson originally conceived the show to be a
dramatization of a fascist takeover of the United States. The network balked; he could only
get the script approved if he cloaked his message in an overlay of science fiction. While the
budget for V was certainly ample—$13 million—it still was not enough for high-tech minia-
ture effects, so the mother ship in the series was a matte painting, not a model.

*Above*: Jane Badler as Diana loses a contact and reveals her inner lizard in V.

*Right top*: Marc Singer as resistance fighter Mike Donovan in V.

*Right bottom*: Charles Mesure and Elizabeth Mitchell in the 2009 television remake of V.

V was unusual for its time because the two-parter ended with no resolution to the conflict. A three-part follow-up, *V: The Final Battle* (1984), which involved a half-human, half-Visitor character named Elizabeth, purported to conclude the story. *V: The Final Battle* has the distinction of being one of the only sequel miniseries in television history to rate higher than the original miniseries. Because of the success of this sequel, a full weekly series version of *V*, featuring most of the original cast, was ordered for the fall of 1984. However, this series had difficulty maintaining the creative tension of the earlier miniseries and lasted for only nineteen episodes. The *V* franchise received a reboot in 2009 with a new series, *V*, which ran on ABC for two seasons. This version postulated that the aliens have been secretly infiltrating the halls of power for decades, and their dramatic landings are simply the beginning of the last act.

**Top**: R2-D2 and C-3PO were inspired in part by the characters of "Tahei" and "Matasichi," down-trodden peasants from Akira Kurosawa's The Hidden Fortress (1958).

**Above**: Harvey Korman and Bea Arthur guest starred in CBS's notorious Star Wars Holiday Special (1978). It must have seemed like a good idea at the time.

**Opposite**: They sure didn't stay unknown!

western" played as a hero's journey, with characters and situations borrowed from Akira Kurasawa's *The Hidden Fortress* and a princess on a dangerous quest accompanied by robot servants. 20th Century Fox finally agreed to put up financing in 1975, but even it failed to see the potential, which is why they allowed Lucas to retain all marketing rights. Even after production began in England there were reports of problems on the set—the British crew didn't get the film or Lucas at all—and production cost overruns.

The first screenings for studio brass, minus most of the special effects or John Williams's dynamic musical score, did little to instill confidence. Even Lucas was starting to believe his dream project was turning into a nightmare. Only Steven Spielberg expressed confidence that the film would be a hit, betting Lucas that *Star Wars* would outgross *Close Encounters of the Third Kind*, which released the same year.

As everybody now knows, the Force was with George Lucas. *Star Wars* became the highest-grossing motion picture ever made to that time. It launched catchphrases, made stars out of Mark Hamill, Carrie Fisher, and Harrison Ford—not to mention the droid R2-D2—and earned six Oscars, plus a nomination for Best Picture.

It also revolutionized the way Hollywood films were made and marketed.

While Lucas always claimed to have envisioned the story of Luke Skywalker as an ongoing saga, even he did not seem to take the film all that seriously at first. That can be the only explanation for *The Star Wars Holiday Special*, a spoofy two-hour special that aired on CBS in 1978, inexplicably starring Harvey Korman, Art Carney, and Bea Arthur. It has never been seen again. The saga continued with *The Empire Strikes Back* (1980), which introduced into the Yoda mythology (puppeteered and voiced by Muppet maven Frank Oz). It also revealed a true bombshell: that villain Darth Vader was really Luke Skywalker's father. It's since become a cliché, but at the time it was truly shocking. The partial cliff-hanger at the end of *The Empire Strikes Back* was resolved in the final chapter, *Return of the Jedi* (1983), which also introduced the diminutive, bear-cub creatures called Ewoks. With Vader dead and the Empire vanquished, the story seemed complete except for the spin-offs (such as television's *Ewok Adventures* in 1983).

More than a decade later, though, there were rumblings that Lucas was returning to the saga with a new trilogy (by the 1990s, trilogies were de rigueur for blockbuster movies—thanks to *Star Wars*). Lucas returned to the director's chair that he had abandoned after the original film to make *Star Wars Episode I: The Phantom Menace* (1999), *Star Wars Episode II: Attack of the Clones* (2002, which spawned two animated series, both titled *Clone Wars*, the first in 2003, with traditional animation, and the second in 2008, with digital animation), and *Star Wars Episode III: Revenge of the Sith* (2005). The prequel trilogy recounts the story of how the evil Empire was formed, and how young Jedi knight Anakin Skywalker transformed into the dark warrior Darth Vader. What's more, the story did it all with spectacular digital effects—including a new, digitally animated, and very mobile Yoda—and advanced the growing medium of high-definition video for the latter two films. (*Phantom Menace* had been shot on 35mm film.) However, by 1999 it was definitely harder to instill the same sense of wonder in an audience, who had seen so many digital wonders on screen previously.

There has been talk over the years about a third *Star Wars* trilogy, one that comes some time in the future, and follows *Return of the Jedi*, but to date there are no definite plans for it. Even without it, the Force will remain part of the collective consciousness of practically everyone in our little corner of the universe.

**Above**: Star Wars' *Death Star trench chase has been often parodied over the years, but when first seen by audiences in 1977, it was pulse-pounding.*

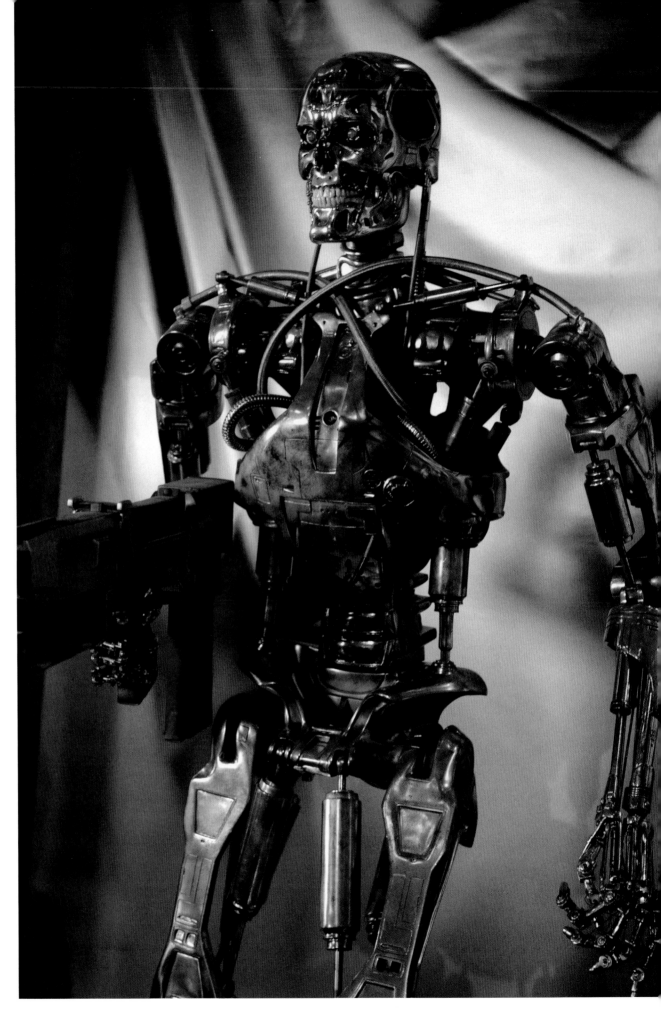

# ALTERNATE TIMES, ALTERNATE REALITIES

# 07

THE SCIENCE FICTION UNIVERSE . . . AND BEYOND

**Above**: *Ostensibly the villain of the first movie,* The Terminator *remains Arnold Schwarzenegger's signature role.*

**Opposite**: The Terminator *without his human costume.*

B y the 1980s, things that traditionally had existed only in the realms of science fiction—lunar landings, missions to the galaxy's outer planets, the existence of space stations, and the use of reentry spacecraft—not only existed, but some of them were becoming commonplace. Sci-fi had to find a new path: it could either go back to the past and change it; it could go further into the future; or it could stay right in the present and show that what we *thought* was reality really was not.

Sci-fi decided to do all three, creating a decade of paradoxical films and television programs that had us both coming and going—and meeting ourselves halfway in between. The "many worlds" interpretation of quantum mechanics, which existed only in theory, had actually become one world that existed on film.

### The Terminator
***"A few years from now, all this, this whole place, everything, it's gone. Just gone."***

It is no exaggeration to say that *The Terminator* (1984), directed by James Cameron, is one of the most influential movies of the late twentieth century. It has been so parodied and quoted that when its star, Arnold Schwarzenegger, went into state politics in California, he was dubbed "The Governator." The film's future backstory starts in 2029, after civilization has been destroyed by a super-computer network called Skynet, a sort of A.I. Old Testament God that decided to wipe out mankind using nuclear weapons instead of a flood. Some survivors fight back, prompting Skynet to send a cyborg Terminator (Schwarzenegger) to 1984 to kill a woman named Sarah Connor (Linda Hamilton), who will eventually have a son named John who will grow up to lead a rebellion against the machines. A human resistance fighter named Kyle Reese (Michael Biehn) follows the Terminator back in time to protect Sarah, and the chase is on. Kyle, of course, paradoxically becomes the father of John, and future history remains exactly as it was.

Schwarzenegger was originally suggested for the role of Reese, but Cameron thought his stiff charm and Austrian accent lent itself more to a machine. (O. J. Simpson had previously been mentioned for the role of the cyborg!) Schwarzenegger rose to the occasion, playing the role with deadpan wit and making the villain of the film its most compelling character. Filmed as a high-end B movie (the budget was only $6.5 million), much of it was shot in real locations in the Los Angeles area, including a shuttered steel mill in the city of Vernon, California, and the Second Street tunnel in downtown L.A. Cinematographer Adam Greenberg utilized a lighting trick to make the high-speed chases shot at night look more dangerous than they were: lights on dimmers were mounted on cars that traveled beside the on-screen vehicles, and the rapid alternation of dimming and raising of the lights made it appear as if the chase vehicles were zooming past street lights much more rapidly than they really were. None of the chases were filmed at speeds greater than 40 miles an hour.

*Above left*: A damaged, but still stoic, cyborg in The Terminator *(1984)*.

*Above right*: Sarah Connor (Linda Hamilton) and Kyle Reese (Michael Biehn) cross timelines to become the parents of John Connor, the central figure in the Terminator *saga.*

*Right*: Robert Patrick—with a lot of digital help—in liquid metal mode as T-1000 in Terminator 2: Judgment Day *(1991)*

The saga of Sarah and John Connor continued on in *Terminator 2: Judgment Day* (1991), one of the first films to utilize computer-generated effects in a major way. That was followed by *Terminator 3: Rise of the Machines* (2003), the last to star Schwarzenegger, and *Terminator: Salvation* (2009), which starred Roland Kickinger, another Austrian-born bodybuilder-turned-actor, who appeared in a digitally created Schwarzenegger "mask" as the Terminator. The saga was brought to television as well, in the 2008 series *Terminator: The Sarah Connor Chronicles*, which ran for two seasons on Fox.

### Back to the Future

*"The way I see it, if you're gonna build a time machine into a car, why not do it with some style?"*

Nothing demonstrates the passage of time more than the fact that one of the biggest laughs in *Back to the Future* upon its release in 1985 was the realization that the time machine was built around a DeLorean DMC-12. The DeLorean was a sleek, faintly futuristic sports car designed and produced by iconoclastic auto executive John DeLorean, who went bankrupt trying to market the car. It was the Edsel of the 1980s, which made it something that would appeal to a mad scientist. Today, DeLorean and his upstart company are all but forgotten, erasing the context for the joke for viewers who weren't around then.

*Above: Inventor Doc Brown (Christopher Lloyd) has time on his hands in* Back to the Future.

*Back to the Future* starred Michael J. Fox as teenager Marty McFly, whose gonzo friend Dr. Emmett Brown (Christopher Lloyd) creates the time machine that shoots Marty back thirty years, where he meets his parents as teenagers. The problem is that his mother is more attracted to him than to his father! Marty has to get his parents together—or else vanish from history—and return to 1985.

Before hitting on the DeLorean idea, director Robert Zemeckis and screenwriter Bob Gale considered making Doc Brown's time machine out of a refrigerator. That carried a couple problems, as Zemeckis explained: "You had to get in and close it before it would start, and then we worried that kids would start locking themselves in refrigerators." Incidentally, John DeLorean himself loved the film and was thrilled his failed car would be immortalized. Actor Eric Stoltz was originally cast as Marty, and almost half of the film had been shot before Zemeckis decided Stoltz was simply wrong for the part and recast Fox in it. The role turned Fox, who was then a television star on *Family Ties*, into a full-fledged movie star.

*Back to the Future*, which was co-produced by Steven Spielberg's Amblin Entertainment, was the top-grossing film of 1985, which meant a trilogy was sure to follow. *Back to the Future Part II* (1989) and *Back to the Future Part III* (1990) were filmed at the same time to take advantage of the reassembled cast (though Crispin Glover, as Marty's

**Above left**: *Marty McFly (Michael J. Fox) and his futuristic hoverboard in* Back to the Future Part II.

**Above right**: *For* Back to the Future Part III, *Doc and Marty went all the way back to the Wild West.*

**Opposite**: *Is he real or digital? Max Headroom.*

nerdy father, was replaced in the sequels by Jeffrey Weisman, made up to look like Glover). *Part II* has Doc and Marty going to 2015 to help Marty's son, only to find upon returning to 1985 that history has radically changed due to an artifact that was accidentally brought back from 1955 in the first film. Some scenes involved the actor either at different ages or in multiple different roles, for which a computer-controlled camera system called Vista Glide was created. The process was essentially an updated double exposure; the moving synchronized camera made it appear as though the actors were interacting with themselves.

*Part III* focused on the past and sent Doc and Marty back to 1885, where Marty meets his immigrant ancestors and Doc meets a woman named Clara (Mary Steenburgen). The DeLorean is destroyed at the end of this film, implying that time will *finally* remain fixed for a while . . . until Doc and Clara arrive in a souped-up, time-traveling railroad engine. Except for Back to the Future: The Ride, at Universal Studios theme parks—one of the first successful "virtual" roller coasters—no other sequels have been made.

### Max Headroom
**"T-t-t-t-tune into Network 23, the network that's a real *mind-blower!*"**
Set in the early twenty-first century, *Max Headroom*, which premiered on ABC in 1987, was a humorously nightmarish allegory about a world controlled by television networks. Structured as a crime drama, the show featured a crusading reporter named Edison Carter (Matt Frewer), who often chased down stories that were politically (or corporately) dangerous, even to his own employer, Network 23. His biggest scoop was the discovery that "blip-verts," rapid-fire sensory-overload ads promoted by the Network's unethical chief Ned Grossberg (Charles Rocket), were actually causing viewers' deaths. To keep the story from getting out, Grossberg tries to prevent Carter from leaving the studio. Carter escapes on a motorcycle but crashes the bike and is rendered comatose. Grossberg's confederate,

**Left**: Max Headroom may look like he's rendered
digitally, but he was really actor Matt Frewer
wearing heavy prosthetic makeup.

**Opposite top**: Chris Young played Bryce Lynch, a
teenaged computer whiz who generates Max
Headroom in the series Max Headroom.

**Opposite bottom left**: The crew of Network 23
in Max Headroom: Edison Carter (Matt Frewer),
Bryce Lynch (Chris Young), Theodora Jones
(Amanda Pays), Murray (Jeffrey Tambor), and
Ben Cheviot (George Coe).

**Opposite bottom right**: Intrepid reporter Edison
Carter becomes gonzo journalist Max Headroom.
Matt Frewer played both.

teenaged genius Bryce Lynch (Chris Young), who is the network's entire research department, uses the accident to Network 23's advantage, extracting Carter's consciousness and
downloading it into a computer. The result is Max Headroom, an unpredictable, sarcastic
cyber-commentator who vaguely resembles Carter and speaks in a variety of ever-changing
pitches and with a pronounced stutter. On occasion, his head explodes as well. Carter
recovers and remains the central human character of the series, with Max as the central
digital character.

The series, which aired for only one season, was based on a 1985 British TV pilot called
*Max Headroom: 20 Minutes into the Future*. In the context of the show, Max was a digital
creation, and many viewers thought they were watching actual digital animation. But Max
was really Frewer filmed in live action before a high-tech graphic background and wearing
stylized prosthetic makeup to make him *look* as if he were animated. The actor's twitchy
movements and some rapid jump-editing aided the illusion. The show had wobbly ratings,
but the character of Max Headroom transcended it (also breaking free of the show's future
setting to become a contemporary personality). He hosted his own talk show, *The Original
Max Talking Headroom Show*, on the cable network Cinemax, and eventually became a
"spokesimage" for Coca-Cola. The name "Max Headroom," incidentally, refers to the last
thing imprinted on Carter's memory before crashing his motorcycle: a sign stating the maxi-
mum headroom, or height clearance, for a parking garage.

## RoboCop
### *"Dead or alive, you're coming with me!"*

*RoboCop* (1987) was something of a rarity for its time: a sci-fi action movie that actually appeared on a lot of critical ten-best-films-of-the-year lists. Set in an unspecified but near future, the film takes place in what is left of Detroit, a city that has become so degraded and crime-ridden that plans are underway to raze it and build a new development called Delta City in its place. The company behind these plans, Omni Consumer Products (OCP), also owns the Detroit police department, which it plans to beef up with a new invention called an Enforcement Droid (ED), a robotic police officer. But when company vice president Dick Jones (Ronny Cox) demonstrates a droid model called ED-209 to corporate executives, the robot malfunctions and kills one of them in cold blood. Instead of the droids, the chairman of OCP opts to go with a different program, one involving the creation of cyborgs, called RoboCops. The body of a policeman named Alexander Murphy (Peter Weller), who was brutally killed in the line of duty, becomes the first RoboCop created through bionics, but who nevertheless retains portions of his humanity.

RoboCop has more on his plate than the common criminals of Detroit. Irate that the ED program was scrapped, Jones murders a rival executive—for which RoboCop cannot touch him, due to a secretly programmed directive preventing him from arresting any OCP brass—and uses ED-209 for protection. RoboCop manages to defeat the metallic droid and reveals to the corporate board the duplicity of Jones, who is summarily fired by his superior and thus made susceptible to being taken down by RoboCop.

The film's primary visual effect was ED-209, which was animated by Phil Tippett in a process that he developed called "go-motion" (as opposed to stop-motion). In go-motion, the figure is filmed one frame at a time, but the figure is moved slightly with rods while the frame is clicked, providing a realistic motion blur. The film's relatively small budget didn't allow for optical matte work, which was the standard method at that time for inserting a different object into a filmed background scene. This forced Tippett to go back to a technique used by Ray Harryhausen, that of rear-projecting the background one frame at a time behind the figure during animation. The scene in which ED-209 is incapacitated by falling down a staircase was shot in real time, with the model tumbling down a miniature flight of stairs, but its violent tantrum upon landing was animated by Tippett.

Because of the violence and blood-and-gore quotient of director Paul Verhoeven's original cut of the film, it was given an X rating, which at the time was a death knell for a commercial movie. Verhoeven toned down some of the carnage and the film was re-rated R. The subsequent franchise included the feature film sequels *RoboCop 2* in 1990 and *RoboCop 3* in 1993, as well as a television series, *RoboCop: The Series* in 1994, and a miniseries,

**Top**: *Starting with films of the 1970s, corporate executives increasingly became the villains of sci-fi films. In RoboCop (1987) Ronny Cox played the malevolent executive.*

**Above**: *The cyborg RoboCop is heat resistant.*

**Opposite**: *Peter Weller as RoboCop.*

**Above**: RoboCop's ED-209, animated by Phil Tippett.

**Left**: The better half of RoboCop (Peter Weller) as seen in RoboCop 2 (1990), with Patricia Charbonneau.

*RoboCop: Prime Directives*, in 2003. In 2011 there was a semi-serious citizens' campaign to erect a statue of RoboCop in Detroit, which is attempting the same sort of revitalization as discussed in the film. Ironically, none of the features were filmed in Detroit at all; *RoboCop* and *RoboCop 2* were filmed largely in Texas and *RoboCop 3* was shot in Atlanta.

**Above***: Lauren Woodland and Eric Pierpoint from the spin-off TV series* Alien Nation.

### Alien Nation
#### *"You humans are very curious to us."*

Capitalizing on the buddy-cop genre made hugely popular by 1987's *Lethal Weapon*, *Alien Nation* (1988) raised the bar even higher in terms of mismatched police partners. Written by Rockne S. O'Bannon and produced by Gale Ann Hurd (who had previously produced *The Terminator* and *Aliens*), the film was a high-concept mix of crime action drama and sci-fi. It contained a strong allegorical theme in which the relationships between the humans and the space aliens stood in for the immigration debate in America. It may not have been the first cop-alien partnership, but it is arguably the best.

The aliens in question come from the planet Tencton and are known on Earth as "Newcomers." They arrived in a gigantic spaceship that landed in the Mojave Desert, and they gravitated toward Los Angeles—despite a severe reaction to seawater, which is a caustic element to their skin—where they integrated into an unwilling society. The Newcomers, who are demeaningly referred to as "slags," are humanoid in appearance but possess large, patterned heads and slits for ears (which frankly make them look like giant Kellogg's Sugar Smacks), and are genetically predisposed for slave labor.

One Newcomer, Sam Francisco (Mandy Patinkin), is not a menial but a police detective. After his partner is killed in a shootout with a Newcomer gang, veteran detective Matthew Sykes (James Caan) volunteers to work alongside Francisco on a homicide case. It's not that he likes the Newcomers or the fact that they are here, but he believes the current case ties in with his old partner's murder. Of course, as the two work together, they begin to develop a mutual respect, even putting themselves in danger for one another, although Sykes persists in calling Sam "George."

The climax of the film involves the pursuit of a Newcomer crime boss named Harcourt (Terrence Stamp), who meets his demise in the ocean and dissolves. To create the dissolving effect, the time-honored method of incorporating Bromo-Seltzer into the makeup was employed. Pockets of Bromo were inserted into the rubber makeup pieces and when wetted, they bubbled and gave the appearance of melting.

*Alien Nation* spawned a Fox television series by the same name in 1989 (which lasted only one season) and was followed by a series of television films in the 1990s.

**Top**: *Terri Treas and Eric Pierpoint from the 1994 television movie Alien Nation: Dark Horizon..*

**Above**: *Kristin Davis, Eric Pierpoint, and Gary Graham in Alien Nation: Body and Soul (1995), one of several TV movies derived from the original feature film.*

**Opposite top**: *Alien Nation (1988) starred James Caan and Mandy Patinkin (left) as an alien no border fence could keep out of California..*

**Opposite bottom**: *James Caan and Mandy Patinkin as the ultimate in mismatched buddy/cops in Alien Nation.*

*Above left: Scott Bakula leaps into the persona of a country veterinarian in* Quantum Leap.

*Above right: Scott Bakula essentially played a different role every week on* Quantum Leap. *Dean Stockwell (seated) remained the same.*

### Quantum Leap
### *"All I do is live someone else's life."*

*Quantum Leap*, which premiered on NBC in 1989, contained elements of several television shows that had preceded it, notably *The Time Tunnel* from 1966, which also involved scientists trapped in time cycles, and *Voyagers* from 1982, in which adventurers traveled back in time to ensure that history unfolded the way it was supposed to at key moments. But the show was also unique in that it was essentially an anthology series starring the same actor each week, but in a different role . . . but not really. Created by Donald P. Bellisario, the series starred Scott Bakula as Dr. Sam Becket, a physicist working on a top-secret time-travel project. When forced to prove his theories or have his project scrapped, Sam puts himself through the Quantum Leap Accelerator and disappears, waking up sometime in the past with a clouded memory and the reflection of a stranger in the mirror. Sam eventually learns from his best friend, Rear Admiral Al "The Observer" Calavicci (Dean Stockwell), who appears to him in holographic form (and whom only Sam can see and hear) that he is trapped in time. Sam will continue to jump from person to person and to varying years, but nearly always the years that have occurred in Sam's own lifetime (in one episode he jumps into his great-grandfather's body). During each leap, he lives that person's life and strives to right whatever wrongs they have experienced, sometimes changing history in small ways (major changes seemed out of bounds).

Over the course of the series Sam jumps into both men and women of varying ages and races, but only he and the viewers at home recognized him as Sam Beckett; within the context of the story, he appears to everyone else as the character. This would occasionally result in problems, such as his not realizing that he is black in a 1955 setting and thus

*Above left*: Time-jumping Dr. Sam Becket (Scott Bakula) sings his heart out for an episode of Quantum Leap.

*Above right*: Scott Bakula (right) sometimes made the ultimate leap—playing a woman—for Quantum Leap.

ignoring segregation rules. Many of the people he meets along the way are historic person-ages, from Lee Harvey Oswald to Elvis Presley, and he even leaps into actual, living famous people who would guest star on the show, such as television's Dr. Ruth Westheimer. The show's emphasis was more on human drama than special effects, though Sam appears to solarize with each new jump (and his catchphrase "Oh, boy" whenever he discovers he is in a new body was ad-libbed by Bakula during one episode and retained for each subsequent one). Throughout the show, Sam expresses the desire to just go home, but the final episode revealed that he always had the ability to jump back into his own body; he simply chose to leap through time and help others. True to his character, rather than return, he decides to jump elsewhere in order to help out his friend Al.

*Quantum Leap* developed quite a following over its five seasons on NBC (technically four a half seasons, since it debuted as a mid-season show), and has become a well-remem-bered cult favorite.

## Total Recall

### *"If I am not me, then who the hell am I?"*

This is your mind; this is your mind affected by Rekall. Any questions?

For Douglas Quaid (Arnold Schwarzenegger), a happily married construction worker in 2084, there are nothing but questions after he visits a company called Rekall to have a virtual Martian vacation implanted in his mind—chiefly, who is he really, and what is reality? *Total Recall* (1990) was directed by Paul Verhoeven and based on Philip K. Dick's short story "We Can Remember It for You Wholesale." It is an effects-laden, existential adventure-cum-spy movie with the quasi-Hitchcockian premise of a man whose life has suddenly been turned inside out, causing him to go on the run—even his wife is out to kill him now that his cover is blown! After seeing a video of himself giving instructions for how to remove a tracking device from his head, Quaid travels to Mars to learn about his secret past, and why it was wiped from his mind like a computer disk's contents.

Quaid learns (or believes he learns) that he was really a former secret agent named Hauser. His erased past, until he rebelled, involved his work on Mars alongside the head of the Mars colony, Vilmos Cohaagen (Ronny Cox, who played a similar role in *RoboCop*), who ruthlessly exploits workers and the planet mining radioactive ore. As Quaid battles Cohaagen, he has to decide whether he was "erased" to keep him from aiding the Martian resistance or turned into a double agent and sent to Earth . . . or whether he is in fact just living out an adventure planted inside his mind by Rekall.

*Total Recall* was filmed in and around Mexico City, with the city's actual rapid transit system representing the subway of the future. The Martian sequences were shot in a soundstage at Mexico City's Churubusco Studios, where large miniatures were used for the environments. The irradiated mutant makeup and animatronics were created by Rob Bottin. Virtually all of the special effects were created through on-set props or miniatures, with digital graphics only being used to create the moving skeletons seen through an X-ray. Speaking of *X*, history for Verhoeven repeated itself as the film was threatened with an X rating because of the overboard violence. As with the case of *RoboCop*, some sci-fi fans felt the Motion Picture Association of America, the rating board for films, treated genre films

**Above**: *Sharon Stone isn't all that happy to see hubby Arnold Schwarzenegger home in* Total Recall.

**Opposite top**: *Implanted memories had side effects in* Total Recall.

**Opposite bottom**: *Arnold Schwarzenegger as Quaid leaping into action in* Total Recall.

**Above**: In Total Recall, the child-like, mutated entity growing out of George (Marshall Bell), who is on Mars, helps Quaid (Arnold Schwarzenegger) recover his past. It could happen.

**Right**: "Mr. Spielberg, I'm ready for my close-up." —T-Rex from Jurassic Park.

differently than "mainstream" movies with similar levels of violence, and that a non-genre film like *Total Recall* would have received an R. Whether this were true or not, Verhoeven did tone down *Total Recall* just enough to receive the all-important R rating. A much more conspiratorial spin-off television series produced in Canada called *Total Recall 2070* aired on Showtime in the United States in 1999. In 2012, a remake of *Total Recall* was released, with Colin Farrell playing the role of Quaid.

### Jurassic Park

***"God creates dinosaurs, God destroys dinosaurs. God creates man, Man destroys God. Man creates dinosaurs."***

As a producer, Steven Spielberg had been interested in dinosaurs for quite some time, but only through the medium of cartoon animation (*The Land before Time* franchise and *We're Back: A Dinosaur's Tale*, both of which he executive-produced). As a director, he assembled a special-effects dream team who brought dinos back like never before in *Jurassic Park* (1993). Based on the novel by Michael Crichton, who co-wrote the script with David Koepp, *Jurassic Park* is about the scientific cloning of a variety of dinosaurs from DNA extracted from prehistoric insects trapped in amber. This monumental discovery was not achieved for scientific study, however; it is to create the ultimate theme park, where visitors can interact with the gigantic creatures. The billionaire behind the plan, John Hammond (Richard Attenborough), thinks it's a great idea. Others, notably paleontologist Alan Grant (Sam Neill), mathematician Ian Malcolm (Jeff Goldblum), and paleobotanist Ellie Satler (Laura Dern), see potential problems. They can't envision the half of it: a park employee who is really in the payroll of a rival of Hammond shuts down the compound security system in order to steal dinosaur embryos. With the protective electronic fencing down, the creatures can run free—and kill.

*Top: Joseph Mazzello, Laura Dern, Sam Neill, and Ariana Richards react to a mighty big lizard in* Jurassic Park.

***Above****: Dr. Alan Grant (Sam Neill) offers a snack to a benign brachiosaurus in* Jurassic Park.

Stan Winston created the animatronic dinosaurs, including a six-foot velociraptor, a long-necked brachiosaurus, a triceratops, and a forty-foot Tyrannosaurus rex made of latex over a fiberglass structure that was operated by puppeteers but which also utilized computerized motion-recording technology so that its movements could be duplicated exactly for multiple takes. The dinosaur puppets were referred to on the set as "Waldos." Marshall Lantieri supervised the on-set dino effects, and to create animated dinosaurs, usually in long shots, Phil Tippett used the go-motion method of animation that he developed at Industrial Light and Magic (ILM), which captured motion blur in each exposed frame of animation, resulting in a heightened sense of realism. But the real innovation came from ILM's Dennis Muren, who was in charge of the digital dinosaurs.

Initially go-motion was going to be the predominant technique until Spielberg became impressed with Muren's digital work, so the responsibility was split up between the two effects. The dinosaur stampede was done all digitally: animator Eric Armstrong created one gallimimus in a run cycle; it was then replicated and the cycles were staggered, resulting in a convincing stampede.

Michael Crichton had already covered the downside of theme parks in *Westworld*, but where that story depicted inexplicably rebellious computers wreaking havoc, *Jurassic Park* featured living, breathing animals acting out their violent natures. A huge hit at the box office, *Jurassic Park* spawned two sequels, 1997's *The Lost World: Jurassic Park*, also directed by Spielberg, and 2001's *Jurassic Park III*, with Joe Johnston in the director's chair. To no one's surprise, the original film also took a Best Visual Effects Oscar. There was another Oscar-related rumor at the time buzzing throughout Hollywood: that Spielberg had cast Attenborough in the film to prevent the veteran actor/director from making a movie of his own—Attenborough's *Gandhi* had beaten out Spielberg's *E.T. the Extra-Terrestrial* for both Best Picture and Best Director Oscars in 1982.

**Above**: *Jeff Goldblum, Richard Shiff, and Vince Vaughn discover stegosaurs in* The Lost World: Jurassic Park *(1997)*.

**Opposite top**: *Effects maestro Stan Winston pets his full-sized creation on the set of* Jurassic Park.

**Opposite bottom**: *The dinos hit the mainland in* The Lost World: Jurassic Park *(1997)*.

# "I'm the Doctor."

The time-traveling adventurer known simply as "the Doctor" has been around for a very long time, both figuratively and literally. Within his ever-evolving storyline, he is said to be in excess of eight hundred years old. *Doctor Who* launched in the U.K. in 1963, and its protagonist is one of the longest-running fictional characters in television history. American viewers were first introduced to the Doctor back in the early 1970s, when the series was syndicated in the United States on mostly PBS-affiliated stations and became a cult hit. Syfy aired many of these early *Doctor Who* seasons (especially the Tom Baker years) during its first few years of existence. In recent years, the Doctor has received a successful reboot from the BBC, with new seasons that have been airing in the States first on Syfy, and later on BBC America.

The Doctor (the "Who" part of the title is not intended to be a name, but the question often asked by other characters: "Doctor who?") is an intergalactic Time Lord from the planet Gallifrey who shuttles through time and space in a device called the TARDIS (Time and Relative Dimension in Space), which looks identical to a 1960s version of the small, public communications kiosks used by the London police force. It appears much larger inside than out. Despite his ability to go virtually anywhere in the universe, he seems to have a special fondness for the planet Earth and spends a good deal of his relative time here, usually in the company of one or more female human companions/assistants. He has saved our planet from destruction or devastation quite a few times. When battling antagonistic life forms, the Doctor eschews conventional weapons, though he does wield a "sonic screwdriver," which can accomplish just about anything.

When *Doctor Who* first began on the BBC in 1963, it was a rather simplistic, videotaped drama that starred William Hartnell as the Doctor and Carole Ann Ford as his granddaughter, Susan. Hartnell, an actor who specialized in playing military officers and authority figures, did not present

*Above: The 1972 TV special* The Three Doctors *brought the various Doctors together. Here the Second Doctor (Patrick Troughton, left) has words with the Third Doctor (Jon Pertwee).*

*Opposite top: The marauding Daleks from* Doctor Who.

*Opposite middle: Tom Baker as the Fourth, and longest-tentured, Doctor.*

*Opposite bottom: William Hartnell (right) originated the character of the Doctor in 1963.*

a warm and fuzzy Doctor; but then, his recurring nemeses the Daleks, hate-filled, robot-like creatures whose battle cry was "Exterminate!" were not very cuddly either. (The series' other long-running antagonist was a megalomaniac called "the Master.") In 1965, Peter Cushing played a more charming, if somewhat dottier, version of the Doctor in the feature film *Dr. Who and the Daleks*, and reprised the role the following year in *Daleks—Invasion Earth: 2150 A.D.*

Illness forced Hartnell out of the role in 1966, by which time the show had become a success, creating a problem for the production staff. The solution was to have the Doctor regenerate into a new body . . . and a new actor. Patrick Troughton became the Second Doctor, playing the role more whimsically. In 1970, the Doctor regenerated into comic actor Jon Pertwee, and four years later regenerated again into the form of Tom Baker.

Baker, who was towering and bushy-haired and possessed a grin like an auto grille, would become the most popular

Doctor, playing the part in eccentric fashion while clad in Victorian dress and a floor-length scarf. In a confluence of sci-fi worlds, author Douglas Adams, creator of *The Hitchhiker's Guide to the Galaxy*, served as script editor and occasional writer for the series in the late 1970s and early 1980s, which is why several *Doctor Who* episodes contain *Hitchhiker's Guide* references. Still shot on videotape and somewhat studio bound, the Tom Baker seasons often utilized multi-episode story arcs, though the settings, effects, and aliens were becoming more elaborate, and the action often took place on a different planet or in an alien spacecraft. After Baker hung up his scarf in 1981, Peter Davison took over, playing the Doctor look as though he just came from the cricket field. He was followed in 1984 by Colin Baker, who presented a supremely self-pleased Doctor in motley; and then in 1987 by Sylvester McCoy, who gave the role a more devious twist.

The original series ended in 1989, but a television movie was produced seven

**Above**: Martha Jones (Freema Agyeman) and the Tenth Doctor (David Tennant), seen outside the TARDIS, were among the series' most popular companion/Doctor teams.

years later, which hoped to introduce the character, finally, to a wide American audience, and ideally, prompt a new series. In the film, which was shot in Vancouver and San Francisco, Sylvester McCoy's Doctor regenerated into Paul McGann (whose Doctor resembled Oscar Wilde) to fight the Master. It aired in the United States on Fox in 1996, but failed to engender much interest. American actor Eric Roberts played the Master.

*Doctor Who* came back with a vengeance in 2005 in a new, filmed series written by Russell T. Davies and produced by BBC Wales, starring Christopher Eccleston as a moody Doctor, and singer/actress Billie Piper as his companion, Rose Tyler. Complete with high-tech special effects and complex storylines, this iteration successfully broke through to the American audience. Unlike the earlier series, which often took place on distant planets (that often looked remarkably like English moors and rock quarries), the reboot concentrated on keeping the Earth safe from marauding aliens. This series introduced a new character: Captain Jack Harkness, a roguish adventurer with the gift of immortality, played by John Barrowman. He was ultimately spun off into his own series, *Torchwood*, in 2006, in which he leads a team of

semi-governmental alien fighters through stories that are a little darker and more character based. The name "Torchwood" is the seemingly arbitrary name given to the secret organization that runs the team, but it becomes less arbitrary when one realizes it is also an anagram of "Doctor Who."

Despite the new series' success in the U.K. and the States, Eccleston wanted out after only one season. He regenerated into the Tenth Doctor, played with loquacious intensity by David Tennant, who, for many, eclipsed even Tom Baker's Fourth Doctor in popularity. During Tennant's tenancy of the TARDIS, another series was spun off: *The Sarah Jane Adventures*, featuring the character of Sarah Jane Smith, who had been the traveling companion of both the Third and Fourth Doctors in the 1970s. This spin-off was targeted to younger viewers. Elisabeth Sladen returned to the role she had created more than thirty years earlier, playing it until her death in 2011.

As of this writing, *Doctor Who* remains in production with a youthful Matt Smith as the Eleventh Doctor, operating a steampunkish TARDIS. It has earned placement in *The Guinness Book of World Records* as the longest-running science fiction program in history.

**Top**: Matt Smith was only twenty-six when cast as the Eleventh Doctor in Doctor Who, making him the youngest actor ever to take the role.

**Above**: The 2005 reboot of Doctor Who starred Christopher Eccleston as the moody Ninth Doctor and Billie Piper as companion Rose Tyler.

ALIENS AMONG US

08

THE SCIENCE FICTION UNIVERSE . . . AND BEYOND

**Above**: David Duchovny as Agent Fox Mulder and Gillian Anderson as Agent Dana Scully investigated The X-Files.

**Opposite**: The X-Files was television's moodiest hour.

By the end of the twentieth century, the universe was becoming a small place, at least in the realm of science fiction. We no longer had to worry about alien life forms coming to Earth: they were already here, walking among us. Anyone traditionally frightened by anyone—or anything—that looked different now had a new cause for concern: the aliens and mutants might just look like *them*. For the first time, television took the lead over feature films in terms of pushing the envelope throughout the decade of the 1990s, resulting in a genuine phenomenon or two.

### The X-Files

*"Trust no one."*

When *The X-Files*, created by Chris Carter, premiered on Fox in September 1993, it was an under-the-radar, moody, sci-fi drama about a special unit of the FBI that handled cases involving the paranormal, UFOs, or other unexplained phenomenon. By the end of its run in 2002, the series had become an entertainment juggernaut: a complex, conspiracy theory/paranoia spy-opera that touched on everything from body transference to alien abductions to political assassination to genetically altered super soldiers. "The truth is out there," the show promised. It just proved awfully hard to find.

FBI agents Fox Mulder (David Duchovny) and Dana Scully (Gillian Anderson) are the primary investigators of the cases in the X-Files, which are overseen by Assistant Director Skinner (Mitch Pileggi). Mulder not only believes that extraterrestrial life was in contact with Earth, he believes that the government knows this and is covering it up. Scully, on the other hand, is far more skeptical—at least initially. As time goes on, the government conspiracy angle takes greater focus, particularly through the appearances of two recurring characters, Cigarette-Smoking Man (William B. Davis) and Well-Manicured Man (John Neville), shadowy figures who appear to know more about the mystery than they explain. When the core of the mystery is revealed, it turns out that it goes all the way back to the infamous alien crash landing of 1947 in Roswell, New Mexico; aliens wanted to colonize the Earth with the help of high-placed earthling assistants. But the plan was thwarted by *another* race of aliens, who attempted to expose the plot.

After seven seasons, Duchovny left the series (explained by having Mulder whisked away on a spaceship). He was replaced by Special Agent John Doggett (Robert Patrick), who would later team up with Agent Monica Reyes (Annabeth Gish), replacing Scully, who was away on maternity leave. Mulder came back periodically in the two final seasons, and by the end of the series, he and Scully—whose genetically engineered baby was being sought by agents—were made fugitives by the government they had served.

*The X-Files* was filmed in Vancouver, B.C., for its first five seasons, giving the episodes built-in atmosphere due to the gray, rainy Canadian climate. It moved to L.A. at the request of Duchovny, who wanted to be closer to his wife. The first feature film, *X-Files* (1998), took advantage of both locations, and recapped the story of the Roswell connection and the attempted takeover of Earth. The main cast was reunited in 2008 for a second feature film, *X-Files: I Want to Believe*, but at that point, the mania over the franchise seemed to have dissipated like the blue haze from Cigarette-Smoking Man.

*Above left*: William B. Davis as the mysterious "Cigarette-Smoking Man," from The X-Files.

*Above right*: In later seasons of The X-Files, Gillian Anderson (center) was joined by Robert Patrick, Mitch Pileggi, Annabeth Gish, James Pickens Jr., and Cary Elwes.

*Left*: Skeptical Agent Scully can't explain away an alien fetus in the X-Files episode "The Erlenmeyer Flask."

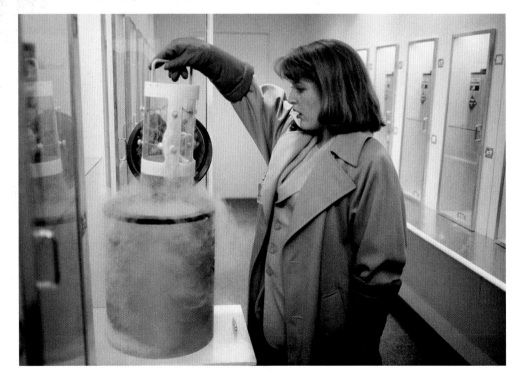

Incidentally, actor William B. Davis, playing Cigarette-Smoking Man, was a non-smoker in real life, just as Anderson, who played the skeptic Scully, was in reality a believer in things supernatural, and Ducovny, who played the believer Mulder, was not.

### Babylon 5
*"It can be a dangerous place, but it's our last, best hope for peace."*

If any sci-fi property fits under the heading "space opera," it is *Babylon 5*, which premiered in syndication in 1994. (Its pilot, a television film called *The Gathering*, had aired the year before.) Imagine *Grand Hotel* to the tenth power, taking place inside a two-and-a-half-million-ton space station; or maybe the United Nations, only with planets instead of countries. Series creator/producer/writer J. Michael Straczynski conceived the show on a huge canvas that would contain one overreaching story arc and several multi-episode subplots. While the show's emphasis was on character dynamics, the special effects were certainly not lacking.

The *Babylon 5* saga begins in the year 2258, some years after a devastating war between Earth and a life-bearing planet twenty-five light-years away started as the result of a misunderstanding. The Babylon Project was an attempt to create intergalactic neutral territory in the form of a space station, where all planetary races could come and work out their differences rather than start more wars. *Babylon 5*, the last remaining station, is large enough to hold a quarter-million beings and welcomes everyone from official diplomats to space drifters.

The show's large cast was initially headed by Michael O'Hare as *Babylon 5*'s commander Jeffrey Sinclair; he left after the first season and was replaced by Bruce Boxleitner as Commander John Sheridan (they didn't even have to change the monograms in the captain's dining room). Other cast members included Claudia Christian; a grown-up Bill Mumy, best remembered as Will Robinson on *Lost in Space*; and the only cast members to appear in every one of the series' 110 episodes, Jerry Doyle, Mila Furan, Richard Biggs, Andreas Katalus, Peter Jurasik and Stephen Furst. Among the many recurring guest stars was *Star Trek*'s Walter Koenig playing a character named Alfred Bester, whom Straczynski named after the noted sci-fi author.

The vividly hued visions of outer space and all the various spacecraft in *Babylon 5* were created with computer graphics, which made the series a pioneer in that area. *Babylon 5* was produced at a budget that was somewhat lower than typical network hour-long programs had at the time, but the producers were smart about stretching resources, using techniques such as redressing the same sets for use as a different location. *Babylon*

*Top: Jerry Doyle, Michael O'Hare, and Claudia Christian in* Babylon 5.

***Above***: *Mira Furlan as the Minbari Ambassador Delenn in* Babylon 5.

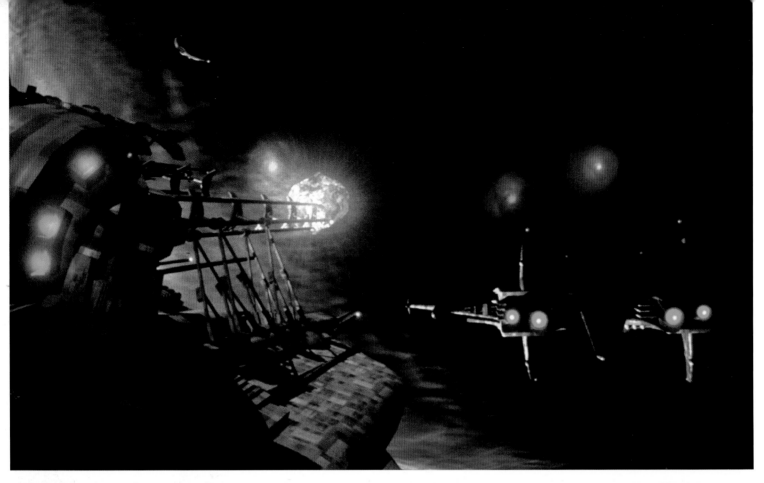

**Top:** *The emphasis in* Babylon 5 *was on the characters, but not at the expense of the spectacle.*

**Above:** *Christopher Judge, Claudia Black, Ben Browder, and Amanda Tapping topped the cast in the tenth, and final, season of* Stargate SG-1.

*5* moved to TNT for its final season, and left the air in 1998, though six television films and the short-lived series *Crusade* (1999), set five years after the end of the *Babylon 5* saga, were spun off from it.

Just as *Babylon 5* is also notable for Straczynski's long-term story planning. While the television norm was to allow a program to evolve and develop on its own as time went on, which in many cases results in a show losing its momentum (and viewers), Straczynski conceived a full, well-developed story arc and did his best to stick with it. *Babylon 5*'s weighty themes of politics, religion, prejudice, and zealotry all played an important part in how the story unfolded.

### Stargate
***"My father found it, 1928; made out of a mineral unlike any found on Earth."***

Even though the feature film *Stargate* was a commercial hit in 1994, its progeny remains better known. Directed by Roland Emmerich from the script he wrote with Dean Devlin, the film starred Kurt Russell and James Spader as a classic sci-fi soldier-versus-scientist in a face-off within an intergalactic adventure with "ancient astronaut" overtones. (In this story, the inhabitants of a distant planet with a culture reminiscent of ancient Egypt came to Earth millennia ago and actually *developed* Egyptian civilization.) The Stargate itself is a mysterious object found in the Egyptian desert, covered in symbols representing space coordinates that have the ability to open up wormholes in space.

Just as *Buffy the Vampire Slayer* had a far greater life on television than in the feature film that introduced the character, the series *Stargate SG-1*, which premiered on Showtime in 1997 and then moved to Syfy in 2002, took the franchise and ran with it. The series began where the movie ended, with Egyptologist Daniel Jackson (Michael Shanks, in the role played by Spader in the film) on the alien planet, now called Abydos, and Colonel Jack O'Neill (Richard Dean Anderson, in the Russell part) leading a team through the Stargate to retrieve him. Jackson has discovered a map rendered in hieroglyphics that shows where other Stargates are located throughout the universe. The Stargates were placed throughout the galaxy by the Ancients, people who settled on Earth millennia ago, leaving clues that have been adapted into earthly myth and legend. The primary antagonists for the first

***Top***: The Stargate unearthed, in the feature film *Stargate*.

***Above***: Kurt Russell (left) represents the military and James Spader stands for science in 1994's *Stargate*.

Above: Richard Dean Anderson (l), Christopher Judge, and the title device of television's Stargate SG-1.

Opposite top: Cleavant Derricks, Kari Wuhrer, and Jerry O'Connell slip in and out of realities in Sliders.

Opposite bottom: Animal/human hybrid Allasandra (Melinda Clark) gets carried away in Sliders.

eight seasons are the Goa'uld, an evil race that once ruled Earth under the guise of ancient mythological deities (and they have the names to prove it, including Anubis, Ba'al, Tanith, and Yu). In the final two seasons, a new alien race called the Ori causes problems.

Because the SG-1 team was military based, the series producers enlisted the cooperation of the United States Air Force, which not only checked scripts for accuracy of terminology and details but allowed some filming to take place outside Cheyenne Mountain in Colorado, which houses the U.S. Air Force's intelligence operation. Stargate SG-1, which was produced primarily in Vancouver, ran for ten seasons and covered a lot of mythology, making it the longest-running primetime science-fiction series produced for American television.

In 2004, the new series, Stargate Atlantis, launched on Syfy and branched the story off to give more focus to the Ancients and their Atlantis connection. It ran for five seasons. A third series, Stargate Universe, premiered on Syfy only nine months after the last episode of Stargate Atlantis aired. The action in this one takes place inside the spaceship Destiny, which was one of the Ancients' fleet that has been traveling the universe.

### Sliders
#### "What if you could find brand-new worlds right here on Earth?"

Most science fiction tales present wormholes as shortcuts through the accepted confines of space and the linear concept of time. The television series Sliders, which premiered on Fox in 1995 and moved to Syfy in 1998, offered a unique wrinkle to the theory: the wormholes are portals to parallel dimensions within the same geographic area but where previously accepted history took a different path.

The device that enables "sliding" in and out of different realities was accidentally created by a brilliant physics grad student named Quinn Mallory (Jerry O'Connell), who lives in San Francisco. The slider device, called the Timer, looks like a handheld remote and counts down the time Quinn is allowed to stay in each reality—a period of time over which he has no control. He makes one successful test run through the glowing vortex before inviting his professor Maximillian Arturo (John Rhys-Davies), and his co-worker, Wade Wells (Sabrina Lloyd), to join him. A has-been soul singer named "Crying Man" Brown (Cleavant Derricks) finds himself in the wrong place at the right time, and he goes through the opened wormhole with the others. Unlike the test run, this slide goes wrong, and they slide into a version of San Francisco suffering through an ice age. A deadly ice storm forces them to slide early, cutting off their route back to their own universe, whereupon the group finds themselves helplessly sliding into one parallel reality after another.

The worlds into which the sliders slide are a compendium of "What if?" alternate realities, including worlds where America lost the Cold War or where dinosaurs still roam the Earth. The various worlds they pass through are sometimes utopias but more often they're dystopic versions of our own world. Often our intrepid team encounters doubles of themselves. In later seasons, the sliders encounter Krogmaggs, warlike creatures faintly Neanderthal in looks but with advanced intellects, who want to take over all iterations of the Earth. The Kromaggs evolve into the show's primary villains; in one reality they enslave

Top: "We're how much over budget?" Kevin Costner in Waterworld.

Above: Producer/star Kevin Costner also did his own stunts in Waterworld.

Right: Jeanne Tripplehorn protects Tina Marjorino (who's showing some attitude of her own) in Waterworld.

**Above**: *Dennis Hopper as the Deacon in* Waterworld.

humans. By those later seasons, though, most of the original cast had left the show, though Quinn was still around, sort of, as Quinn 2, a combination of Quinn and another slider and played by Robert Floyd. Cleavant Derricks as Crying Man was the only original slider to make it all the way through the final episode, when (but where exactly?) "Slidology," a cult-ish religion based on the sliders, has been introduced.

*Sliders* left the air in 2000, and since no resolution was offered to the saga, one can assume either that they are still sliding or are satisfied with the countless fan fiction takes on this series that can be found on the Internet.

### Waterworld

#### *"Dry land is not just our destination, it is our destiny!"*

Even before its release in 1995, the critics were gunning for *Waterworld*. The film, which starred and was produced by Kevin Costner, cost a record $175 million, had been in production for a near-record eighteen months, and was known as a troubled production whose director, Kevin Reynolds, bailed out after a dispute with Costner. Pundits delighted in calling it *Fishtar* and *Kevin's Gate*—riffs on the infamously self-indulgent and wildly expensive Hollywood bombs *Ishtar* and *Heaven's Gate*—and invoked every variation imaginable of the phrase "all wet." The thing is, *Waterworld* really isn't that bad.

The film is set in the twenty-fifth century, after the polar ice caps have melted and flooded the Earth. People called Atollers are confined to small islands, while ruthless sea pirates called Smokers rule the rest of the world. Their leader, Deacon (Dennis Hopper), captain of an ancient rusted-out tanker called the *Deez*, is looking for a small child named Enola (Tina Majorino), who has a birthmark on her back that looks like a map to dry land. Enola is cared for by a woman named Helen (Jeanne Tripplehorn), but it takes the arrival of the Mariner (Costner) to fend off the Smokers. Traveling the waters on a towering trimaran, the Mariner has evolved (or mutated) to match the new environment: he has webbed feet and gills.

The Deacon manages to kidnap Enola, who is ultimately rescued by the Mariner and Helen. They kill the Deacon and blow up the *Deez* (which turns out to be the ruins of the *Exxon Valdez* . . . maybe you had to have been there) and then fashion a hot-air balloon to escape. Translating the birthmark on Enola's back, the Mariner gets them to Dryland, which is the top of Mount Everest! There Helen and Enola settle in the new land, but the Mariner, a creature of both dry land and water, moves on.

**Above**: *Filming* Waterworld *on the ocean, without movie trickery, meant that the cast and crew were at the mercy of the weather.*

*Waterworld* was filmed off Rawaikae Harbor in Hawaii, and virtually all of its sets, from the Mariner's trimaran to the enormous artificial atoll floating in the water, were full-sized practical ones, not miniatures. The primary computer-generated imagery used in the film was said to be at Costner's insistence, to beef up his thinning hair. The atoll set was a quarter mile in circumference and made from one thousand tons of steel. While it managed to stay afloat, an elaborate thirty-five-foot-tall slave-colony set sank into the waters. Filming on the water was, in large part, the reason for the film's schedule overruns, since constantly changing sky and water conditions made lighting continuity a challenge. The cast and crew also had to endure sudden squalls that would come out of nowhere, one such storm whipped up during a shot in which Costner was tied to a mast of his trimaran; unable to get down, he had to ride out the storm lashed to the mast.

*Waterworld* received some good notices amid the sniping and was a hit overseas. Given all the problems, it was not a good candidate for a sequel. A stunt-show adaptation, though, has played successfully at Universal Studios theme parks worldwide, and the initial judgment of it seems to be belied by the decent ratings *Waterworld* earned from airings on Syfy and other television networks. Occasionally, it's the critics who are all wet.

### The Fifth Element
***"Me fifth element—supreme being. Me protect you."***
Once every five thousand years three planets eclipse simultaneously, which signals the opening of a portal into an alternate dimension and unleashes the "Great Evil" upon Earth . . . and in the year 2263, it's about to open again. The only defense is the Divine Light generated by bringing together four ancient stones representing the basic earthly elements—earth, wind, fire, and water—with the Fifth Element, which is a human kept in a sarcophagus in Egypt. The stones were planted on Earth by aliens called the Mondoshawans, who return to fight the Great Evil every time it appears with the aid of an earthly representative. This time, though, the Great Evil has its own human representative, Zorg (Gary Oldman), who unleashes nasty aliens called Mangalores to defeat the Mondoshawans. They almost do, but enough of the Fifth Element is recovered to clone a new body, a woman named Leeloo (Mila Jovovich). Disoriented by the experience, Leeloo flees, landing in a flying taxicab driven by a former special-ops agent named Dallas (Bruce Willis). And this is just the set-up!

**Top**: Leeloo (Mila Jovovich) is brought to life in The Fifth Element.

**Above**: High priest Vito (Ian Holm, center) is at the mercy of Mandalore warriors in The Fifth Element.

THE SCIENCE FICTION UNIVERSE . . . AND BEYOND

Suddenly thrust into the battle for Earth's survival, Dallas helps Leeloo reunite the elements, defeating both Zorg and neutralizing the Great Evil—which manifested itself into a blazing black fireball heading for the Earth—by turning it into a second moon. And naturally, along the way Dallas and Leeloo have fallen in love . . . which may be the *true* Fifth Element.

Directed by Luc Besson and based on a story he dreamed up as a teenager, *The Fifth Element* (1997) was a French production that was set in a futuristic version of New York and shot mostly in England. A massive model of twenty-third-century New York, composed of twenty-two buildings with an average height of sixteen feet, filled two soundstages at Pinewood Studios outside London. Meanwhile, L.A.'s Digital Domain handled the computer graphics, including the Great Evil and the film's flying vehicles, some of which were whimsically designed, to create a Big Apple that is just as traffic clogged in the air as it ever was on the ground. The effects shop spent a year pre-visualizing, storyboarding, and designing the future city, and in its execution set a record for the time by compositing more than eighty individual elements into one frame of film.

French comics artists Jean-Claude Mézières, who created the sci-fi comic *Valérian and Laureline*, and Jean "Moebius" Girard contributed to the design of the film, while fashion designer Jean-Paul Gaultier designed the film's costumes, notably Leel's memorably revealing looks.

### Men in Black
***"At any given time there are approximately fifteen hundred aliens on the planet, most of them right here in Manhattan."***

MIB—Men in Black—might be the only governmental agency that actually works. Under the guise of a nonexistent division of the Immigration and Naturalization Service, the Men in Black keep the world safe for safe aliens—who live on the planet in disguise—and rid the world of dangerous aliens—who also live on the planet in disguise—all the while keeping the knowledge of any of it from the general public, often through the use of a memory-erasing device.

Director Barry Sonnenfield's 1997 adaptation of the eponymous comic book, scripted by Ed Solomon, was the ultimate sci-fi/comedy/buddy-cop film. MIB Agent K (Tommy Lee Jones) is in need of a new partner and decides that New York cop James Edwards III (Will Smith) is just the man. He convinces Smith to team up, despite the huge personality differences: Edwards—now Agent J—is hip and loose, while K is as tight as a sailor's knot. They dress alike in regulation MIB garb: black suits, skinny ties, and cool Ray-Ban shades. The two have to track a malicious "Bug" alien, which has taken over the body of a farmer named Edgar (Vincent D'Onofrio) in order to obtain an object called the Galaxy, which will help them win a war against another alien race. The clock is ticking, too, since yet another alien race, the Arquillians, is willing to destroy Earth if that's what it takes to make sure the Bugs don't get their hands on the Galaxy. They give the MIB a day to recover the object, or else.

***Above****: Leeloo (Mila Jovovich) tries to escape her creation, but instead propels herself into the action of* The Fifth Element.

***Opposite top****: Traffic jams in the twenty-third century, according to* The Fifth Element.

***Opposite bottom****: Dallas (Bruce Willis) just wants another fare, but ends up battling for the world's survival in* The Fifth Element.

Clint Eastwood was originally sought for the role of Agent K, but he passed on the script. The elaborate alien effects for the film, many of which involve aliens inhabiting humans, were a combination of animatronic puppets, miniatures, digital animation, and special makeup by Rick Baker, whose work on *Men in Black* won an Oscar. This mingling of techniques was highlighted by the alien character "Mikey," for which actor John Alexander wore a 150-pound suit with a computer-controlled head (out of which he couldn't see); when the character was required to suddenly roar, it was replaced by computer animation by Industrial Light and Magic. Miniatures were used for the climactic sequence depicting a spaceship crashing through the Unisphere in New York's Flushing Meadows, which ironically (or intentionally) had been the site of the 1939 New York World's Fair that offered a vision of "The World of Tomorrow."

Even though Agent K has his memory wiped and is retired at the end of *Men in Black* (1997), he is coerced back into the MIB for *Men in Black II* (2002), once more to help Agent J save the Earth from destruction. One of J's partners is Frank the Pug, an alien disguised as a pug dog, who put in an appearance in the original film; Frank the Pug is given a featured role in the sequel. The franchise is continuing with *Men in Black III*, once again featuring Jones and Smith. This time, Agent J must travel back in time to the 1960s to prevent Agent K's assassination.

### Farscape
#### "I'm nobody's puppet!"

Shot in Australia with a mostly local cast, *Farscape*, which premiered in 1999, was a quirky and very well-reviewed sci-fi adventure set on board what has to be the most unique spaceship of all time: a gigantic living creature called Moya, which is part organism and part machine, and which broke free of the control of a militaristic organization called the Peacekeepers. The inhabitants of Moya are a disparate bunch: D'Argo (Anthony Simcoe), a huge alien warrior; Rygel (a creation of Jim Henson's Creature Shop, voiced by Jonathan Hardy), a one-time emperor; and Zhaan (Virginia Hey), a robin's-egg-blue, bald, but otherwise beautiful plant-based priestess, were all once rebel prisoners of the Peacekeepers. With them are the human-appearing Aeryn Sun (Claudia Black), a former Peacekeeper who defied the organization, and the show's anchor, Commander John Crichton (Ben Browder), a twentieth-century astronaut who was sucked through a wormhole while testing an experimental craft called *Farscape*. A reluctant, somewhat bumbling rebel, Crichton wants to find

**Top**: *Tommy Lee Jones as Agent K and Richard Hamilton as Agent D find the aliens in* Men in Black.

**Above**: *Mr. Jones and Mr. Smith, the* Men in Black.

**Top**: A spaceship crashes into the Unisphere in New York in Men in Black.

**Above left**: Aliens of all stripes from Men in Black II (2002).

**Above right**: Puppeteer/actor Tim Blaney provided the voice of Frank the Pug in Men in Black II.

a way back to Earth, but he also succumbs to the charms of Aeryn as they try to stay out of the clutches of the Peacekeepers.

Created by Rockne S. O'Bannon and Brian Henson, and produced by Jim Henson Productions and Hallmark Entertainment, *Farscape* was a lavish, expensive show with highly sophisticated special effects for a TV series. Rygel (who despite his protests really *was* a puppet, one that looked a bit like a crawfish on steroids) existed in two formats: an on-set Muppet with animatronic facial controls and lip movements that were operated through a multi-axial cable joystick, and a completely digital version used for shots in which he is shown flying on his "hover throne." The editorial team was careful, though, never to let the two different versions be intercut together. Moya's Pilot, on the other hand, was a large-scale animatronic figure, without any traditional puppeteering.

The action of the series was also structured to cover one long, sweeping story arc that continued from one season to the next. It developed an immediate cult following after its premiere in the United States on Syfy and in Australia on Nine Network, so much so that when the plug was pulled on the show at the end of its fourth season—the last episode of which ended with a "To Be Continued" message—fans immediately launched a letter-writing campaign to bring it back. It worked; a two-part miniseries titled *Farscape: The Peacekeeper Wars* aired on Syfy in 2004, concluding the ongoing saga.

### The Iron Giant
*"I am not a gun."*

The animated feature film *The Iron Giant* is renowned for being a textbook example of how to make a groundbreaking animated feature, and then how to throw it away through bad marketing. Despite its being one of the best-reviewed movies of 1999, it was a commercial flop in the United States, a fact that the filmmakers, along with several critics, blamed on Warner Bros.' rescheduling of the picture's release date at the last minute in order to concentrate on promoting its steampunkish cowboy adventure *The Wild Wild West*.

Director Brad Bird turned his attention to *The Iron Giant* after his pitch for an animated sci-fi film called *Ray Gunn* was rejected. Loosely based on Ted Hughes's book *The Iron Man*, the film is a throwback to the kind of sci-fi stories and themes that proliferated in the 1950s. Set in 1957, the film begins with the crash landing of the Iron Giant (voiced by Vin Diesel) off the coast of Maine. Designed as a weapon but somehow possessing a soul, the Giant is discovered by a young, fatherless boy named Hogarth (Eli Marienthal), who manages to strike up a friendship with the gigantic creature. He invites the Giant home but discovers he is rather hard to hide. The Giant has left enough traces of his presence to alert a government agent, who is tracking him and in turn alerts the military. Despite Hogarth's best efforts to protect his friend, the military eventually catches up with the robot, who is unable to control his built-in defense mechanisms and fights back. The government agent imagines himself to be in charge of the situation and forces the launch of a nuclear missile from an offshore carrier, realizing too late that the weapon will also wipe out everybody in the town! The Giant flies up to the missile and intercepts it in the air, sacrificing himself. But the Giant is self-repairing, and his artificial brain, which has been blasted to Iceland, begins summoning widespread pieces for reassembly.

*Above*: Anthony Simcoe and Ben Browder in Farscape.

*Opposite top*: Peacekeeper commander Scorpius (Wayne Pygram) gets the drop on Crichton (Ben Browder) in Farscape.

*Opposite bottom*: Ben Browder, as astronaut John Crichton, shoots through a wormhole and ends up on the Moya in Farscape.

**Top**: Hogarth and the mysterious Giant inspect each other in Brad Bird's The Iron Giant.

**Above**: The military in The Iron Giant never met an alien entity it didn't imprison.

**Right**: The character of the Giant in The Iron Giant was computer animated, but made to look hand-drawn.

Unlike all the other characters in the film, the character of the Iron Giant was animated digitally. This was done in part because of the complexity of the character design, but also so he would seem organically different in movement from the other characters. Even so, the CG animation was put through an additional rendering process that gave it a distinct outline, so that it *looked* like traditional animation. While the film was steeped in Cold War atmosphere, it is never made explicit as to whether the Giant is a secret Soviet weapon, a robot from outer space, or something else. Despite the bungled marketing campaign in the United States, the film did well internationally.

### The Matrix
*"The answer is out there, Neo, and it's looking for you, and it will find you if you want it to."*

A complex, bizarre, cyberpunk-powered variation about the nature of genuine reality—is it that which we live or that which we dream?—*The Matrix* (1998) pondered the question of reality while also offering gravity-defying Hong Kong–style martial-arts action sequences. In the film a computer hacker named Thomas (Keanu Reeves), whose online alias is "Neo," begins to see references on his computer that refer to "the Matrix," and grows curious. A fellow hacker named Trinity (Carrie-Anne Moss) tells him that a man named Morpheus (Laurence Fishburne) can provide him with the truth; but sinister figures intercept him to warn him about contact with Morpheus. Neo ignores them and meets up with Morpheus, who provides him with a choice between two pills: the blue pill will change nothing, and the red will show him the truth.

Opting for the red pill, he learns that it is really the year 2199, a time when super computers control everything. The life he previously knew is actually the Matrix, a reality generated by the computer and implanted into humans to keep them placid. Humans are cultivated by the machines for an energy source. Morpheus and Trinity have freed themselves from the Matrix and are part of the rebellion against the machines. The rebellion's base an underground city called Zion, the last human stronghold,. Neo joins the rebellion, and there is debate about whether or not he is "The One," mankind's "savior." As Neo gains power he learns how to combat and defeat the Matrix's defenders.

The principal cast spent four months training with martial arts master and Hong Kong director Yuen Woo-ping on kung fu and wire stunt work. The visible wires, of course, would later be digitally erased, making it appear as if the actors were really running up walls or hovering in air. The action scenes were shot in "bullet-time": the scene was shot normally, and the images fed into a computer using a laser-guided tracking system that mapped out the camera movements. Following the map, a series of still cameras were set up and the action repeated. The photos from this were scanned digitally, the action connected by digital in-between images, and then the sequence manipulated to create physics-busting

**Above***: Hogarth and the Giant become fast friends in* The Iron Giant.

**Above**: Neo (Keanu Reeves) is offered a reality-defining choice in The Matrix.

**Left**: The Matrix code from The Matrix.

**Below left**: Morpheus (Laurence Fishburne) in action in The Matrix.

**Below right**: An example of "bullet-time" photography from The Matrix.

imagery. The scenes in which time appears to slow down to nothing were filmed with ultra-high-speed cameras that passed film through at 12,000 frames per second!

For the dramatic shootout in the lobby of the office building, a huge set was built on a soundstage, and behind it the image of the city was projected through a large transparency called a Translight. The resulting background image was forty-two feet high and one hundred forty feet long! Written and directed by Andy and Larry Wachowski, *The Matrix* was hugely successful, which by 1999 meant it had earned its trilogy stripes. *The Matrix Reloaded* and *The Matrix Revolutions* were shot simultaneously in 2001 and into 2002, and both films were released in 2003.

*Above*: Trinity (Carrie-Anne Moss) is Neo's mentor and love interest in The Matrix.

*Left*: Neo (Keanu Reeves) is pursued by an army of Agent Smiths (Hugo Weaving) in The Matrix Reloaded (2003).

### Steven Spielberg Presents Taken

*"Can you imagine what would have happened to people if, in 1947, they thought that we were going to be invaded by aliens?"*

Since so much of American UFO lore begins with the summer 1947 incident at Roswell, New Mexico, in which . . . *something* . . . crash-landed on a ranch near the city, it is fitting that Steven Spielberg's epic ten-part miniseries *Steven Spielberg Presents Taken* (2002) begins there as well. Costing approximately $40 million, *Taken*, which initially aired on Syfy in December 2002, was a hugely ambitious undertaking for television. It presented a James A. Michener–sized saga that spanned a half century and chronicled the multigenerational lives of three separate families, each of whom were affected by the Roswell incident. While what really came down at Roswell is still hotly debated in the real world, *Taken* brooks no argument: it was a UFO, and the government has covered it up.

The three central families are the Keys (an interesting choice of name in that it echoes the moniker of the government agent from Spielberg's *E.T.*), the Clarkes, and the Crawfords. The links between these families are threaded in the first episode, which finds World War II pilot Russell Keys (Steve Burton) haunted by shadowy memories of an alien abduction and experimentation during the war. Meanwhile, another military man, Captain Owen Crawford (Joel Gretsch) discovers the crashed UFO at Roswell, and comes into possession of "the artifact," a mysterious piece of alien technology that he ruthlessly uses to achieve control of the UFO Project studying the Roswell incident, and ultimately leads to the cover-up.

Crawford realizes that one of the UFO's crew has survived the crash. That alien, having assumed human form and adopted the name John, is taken in and protected by a woman named Sally Clarke (Catherine Dent), who becomes pregnant by him. All of their children and grandchildren—including Allie Keys (Dakota Fanning), Russell's great-grandaughter, who is half human and half alien—continue the story. What is revealed throughout the course of the saga is that the Alien Visitors, as they are identified, have been abducting humans and implanting tracking devices into them for decades. The goal is to find suitable mating partners, which the aliens hope will genetically improve their amoral characters (!).

Scripted solely by Leslie Bohem (who was co-executive producer along with Spielberg), and boasting of ten directors, including Tobe Hooper (*Poltergeist*), *Taken* was filmed in British Columbia. Whenever possible the miniseries utilized actual details of alleged genuine alien abductions, including a reference to Barney and Betty Hill, a New Hampshire couple who claimed to have been abducted into a UFO in 1961. The show's UFO Project also echoes the real life "Project Mogul," a top-secret weather balloon operation that is, according to the government, officially the source of the Roswell crash debris.

One of the most successful programs ever to air on Syfy, *Taken* went on to win that year's Emmy for Outstanding Miniseries.

**Above**: *The saga of* Steven Spielberg Presents Taken *spanned seven decades, ending in 2002 with Adam Kaufman, Ryan Hurst, Dakota Fanning, and Emily Berg.*

**Opposite top**: *Sam Crawford (Ryan Merriman) discovers a human/alien hybrid in* Taken.

**Opposite bottom**: *Captain Owen Crawford (Joel Gretsh) learns the truth about Roswell early on in* Taken.

THE SCIENCE FICTION UNIVERSE . . . AND BEYOND

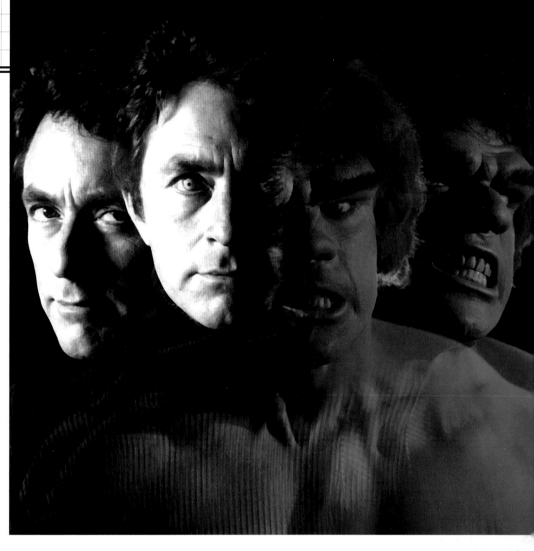

**Above left**: Nicholas Hammond played Peter Parker, but most of the Spidey scenes featured stuntman Fred Waugh, in TV's The Amazing Spider-Man.

**Above right**: Bill Bixby "hulking out" into Lou Ferrigno in television's The Incredible Hulk.

There had been talk of a Spider-Man feature film for the better part of two decades, with numerous story treatments swinging through Hollywood. Finally, in 2001, the film went into production, under the direction of Sam Raimi. *Spider-Man* (2002) starred Tobey Maguire as the high school nerd who gets bit by a radioactive spider in a science lab, and as a result, develops spider powers and senses. It was a huge hit that allowed not only for multiple sequels of its own but helped greenlight *Daredevil* (2003), which depicted an attorney who loses his sight from exposure to radioactive material but gains increased sensitivity in his other senses; and two feature film adaptations of the Hulk, the first (cleverly) titled *Hulk*, which came out in 2003, and the second, *The Incredible Hulk*, a 2008 reboot. Both featured digitally generated Hulks, though for the reboot, performance-capture technology provided a basis upon which to animate the character.

Marvel's seminal superhero comic *The Fantastic Four*, about a quartet of astronauts who develop strange abilities after exposure to cosmic rays, finally got a releasable big screen treatment in 2005; a sequel, *Fantastic Four: Rise of the Silver Surfer*, followed in 2007, combining the four with the surfboard-riding, alien

herald for a world-consuming entity called Galactus. *Iron Man*, about a billionaire playboy military contractor who builds a near-invincible flying metal suit (which was digitally animated), was a surprise success in 2008—even for a superhero movie; the first sequel, *Iron Man 2*, followed in 2010.

Clearly audiences couldn't get enough of superheroes; one of television's top-rated shows during this time was simply called *Heroes* (2006–10), which followed the changing lives of a variety of characters who begin to realize they possessed superhuman abilities. A shadowy organization called "The Company" seeks to monitor their activities and those of superhumans like them. Created by Tim Kring, the NBC series was structured a bit like a graphic novel, with each episode representing one chapter of an overall sweeping story arc (and each season had its own defining theme: "Genesis," "Generations," "Villains," and "Redemption"). Meanwhile Syfy's *Alphas* presents an action-oriented, character-based take on the superhero genre.

The theatrically released film *Watchmen*, based on DC's 1985 pioneering graphic novel, spent years in development hell, but by the time the moody, violent, noirpunkish, alternate-reality adventure was finally released in 2009, the buzz about

it had died down. Like 2010's *Kick-Ass*, a dark non-sci-fi adventure about a teenage wannabe superhero and an eleven-year-old vigilante whose vocabulary would have shocked Richard Pryor, the film was rated R. More traditional was *Green Lantern* (2011), based on the DC character, an earthly member of an intergalactic force called the Guardians of the Universe.

Captain America, who had several cinematic false starts going back to a 1945 serial adaptation that had nothing to do with the comic book mythology, returned to the big screen in 2011 in *Captain America: The First Avenger*. The film recounted the original story of Steve Rogers, a 4-F weakling during World War II, who is turned into

a super soldier through a secret experiment utilizing a special serum and radiation treatment. Rogers becomes a superhero instead. Like the recent adaptations of *The Incredible Hulk*, *Iron Man* and 2011's *Thor* (another non-sci-fi superhero), *Captain America: The First Avenger* is in one sense a teaser for the long awaited, "ultimate" superhero film, *The Avengers* (2012).

Why did it take superhero movies so long to gain a foothold in Hollywood? In large part, the industry had to wait until the visual effects technology could catch up with the imaginative visions offered by the comic book artists and writers. Like aliens on Earth, however, now that superhero films are here, they are all but taking over.

*Top*: A digitally animated Hulk in The Incredible Hulk *(2008)*.

*Above left*: One of Marvel's least-adapted major characters, the Silver Surfer, was the star of Fantastic Four: Rise of the Silver Surfer.

*Above right*: Robert Downey Jr., as Tony Stark a.k.a. Iron Man, in 2010's Iron Man 2.

*Above*: Spider-Man *finally swung into movie theaters in 2002.*

*Right*: A paramilitary Cap (Chris Evans) in Captain America: the First Avenger (2011).

# THE SCIENCE FICTION
# CULTURE
# 09

Yesterday's science fiction has become today's science fact, so much so that it is often difficult to differentiate between the two. Fiction's privately built spaceships have become reality's privately financed rocket launches. Fiction's speculation of life on other planets has become reality's statistical probability, as scientists continue to identify "Goldilocks planets," or those that are neither too close nor too far from their sun to contain water but are just right—which means they *might* sustain life. Fiction's imaginings about artificial intelligence have become reality's computer brain "Watson."

For many people, the phrase "the twenty-first century" still carries with it the hint of futurism, yet here it is. And in its first decade, sci-fi filmmaking has become as familiar as a favorite chair, characterized only by the kinds of now-limitless visual wonderment that is available at the fingertips of today's filmmakers.

### Epoch
***"The public has been told it's a weather phenomenon and that's all they need to know."***

Tautly tying together a half-dozen different sci-fi conventions—a mysterious artifact left on Earth by aliens, the eternal conflict between military might and scientific study, government conspiracy, neo–Cold War struggles, and an end-of-the-world scenario—there is not much the television film *Epoch* (2001) leaves out.

*Epoch* premiered as part of Syfy's ongoing Saturday Original Movie franchise. Over the last decade or so, Syfy has made roughly two hundred original movies, generally premiering two per month on alternating Saturday nights throughout the year. Thematically, Syfy's original movies run the gamut from traditional creature features (*Manticore*; *Yeti*; *Ogre*) to world-in-jeopardy disaster films (*Ice Twisters*; *Black Hole*) to action films with environmental themes (*Snakehead Terror*; *Mansquito*). Some fall into the high-camp arena (*Alien Apocalypse* and Roger Corman's *Sharktopus*), while others involve aliens and space exploration (*Crimson Force*; *Star Runners*). There are even originally produced theatrical movie sequels (the *Lake Placid* and *Anaconda* franchises). *Epoch* was one of Syfy's movie franchise's more serious-minded and more purely science fiction original movies.

*Epoch* begins four billion years ago (!) when a mysterious object rockets through space and crash-lands on Earth. Then, in modern-day Bhutan, a small country nestled between India and China, a mysterious monolith suddenly emerges from the ground. Resembling an explosion cast in rock, its emergence causes enough of a ruckus on seismic equipment to suggest a nuclear device has gone off, but nobody knows what it is. The U.S. government takes charge in investigating it, knowing that they are stepping into a tricky political minefield, since the monolith—called the Toros—is close to the Chinese border. Engineer and analytical wizard Mason Rand (David Keith) and NSA official Dr. K.C. Czaban (Stephanie Niznik) are dispatched to the site, in the company of the military, led by by-the-book Captain Tower (Brian Thompson). The Chinese are also interested in the object and attempt to infiltrate the site, which causes tensions back in Washington.

***Above***: *David Keith and Stephanie Niznik in* Epoch.

***Opposite***: *Rand (David Keith) makes his way through the monolith in* Epoch.

*Above: Rand (David Keith) and Dr. Czaban (Stephanie Niznik) try to defuse a bomb in* Epoch.

*Opposite top: Adam Baldwin, Alan Tudyk, Nathan Fillion, and Gina Torres were the core crew of the* Serenity *in* Firefly.

*Opposite bottom left: River Tam (Summer Glau) was a fugitive on board the* Serenity *in* Firefly.

*Opposite bottom right:* Serenity, *the feature film version of TV's* Firefly, *was released in 2005.*

Rand and Czaban gain access inside the monolith, which is inhabited by an energy force that has power over illness and death, and try to figure out its meaning and existence. The military, however, with the blessing of the president, wants to nuke it, particularly when it begins emitting a thick cloud that will cover the Earth and create a nuclear winter that will choke out all life within a matter of months. The nuke is set and goes off, but the Toros absorbs the shock, collapsing into itself and releasing the energy force, which blows away the cloud cover. Rand theorizes that the purpose of the Toros was to "re-terraform" the Earth, bringing one evolutionary epoch to a sudden end so that another can begin. The implication is that the monolith, rather than the popularly held theory of a meteor crash, is what wiped out the dinosaurs. And while he has no idea why, he believes that it changed its mind at the last minute, deciding the human race has a little more evolution left in them.

Produced independently by Unified Film Organization (UFO) on a $2 million budget, *Epoch* aired as a Syfy original movie in November 2001 and earned the best ratings for a Syfy original movie at the time. A sequel, *Epoch: Evolution*, in which *two* Toroses burst forth from the newly spiritualized Earth, aired in 2003.

### Firefly

**"Here's how it is: the Earth got used up, so we moved out and terraformed a whole new galaxy of Earths."**

Given that science fiction and the western are the cinema's first true genres, their marriage should not be all that surprising. The 2002 Fox series *Firefly*, though not the first or only sci-fi western, is perhaps the best known. Created by Joss Whedon, *Firefly* is a genuine space western, set in the year 2517 but complete with horses and six-shooters in addition to insectoid spaceships. In fact, Whedon's stated inspiration was John Ford's classic western *Stagecoach*, about a disparate assortment of travelers riding through dangerous territory together.

*Firefly* centered on a similar group of outcasts aboard the *Serenity*, a Firefly-class spaceship, so called because it somewhat resembles a gigantic firefly; the rear engine of the craft lights up when the ship accelerates. The *Serenity*'s captain, Mal Reynolds (Nathan Fillion), fought against the Sino-American Alliance of Central Planets, which was attempting to bring all newly formed planets under its rule. Having fought on the losing side, Reynolds now steers clear of the Alliance, keeping the *Serenity* out of sight at the edges of the galaxy.

The ship's nine-member crew includes Zoe Washburn (Gina Torres), who fought alongside Reynolds in the war and is now his lieutenant; Zoe's husband, "Wash" Washburn (Alan Tudyk), the *Serenity*'s pilot; Jayne Cobb (Adam Baldwin), a brawny mercenary who initially fought against Reynolds until getting a better offer; Inara Sera (Morena Baccarin), a professional "Companion" (courtesan); Kaylee Frye (Jewel Staite), the *Serenity*'s self-taught

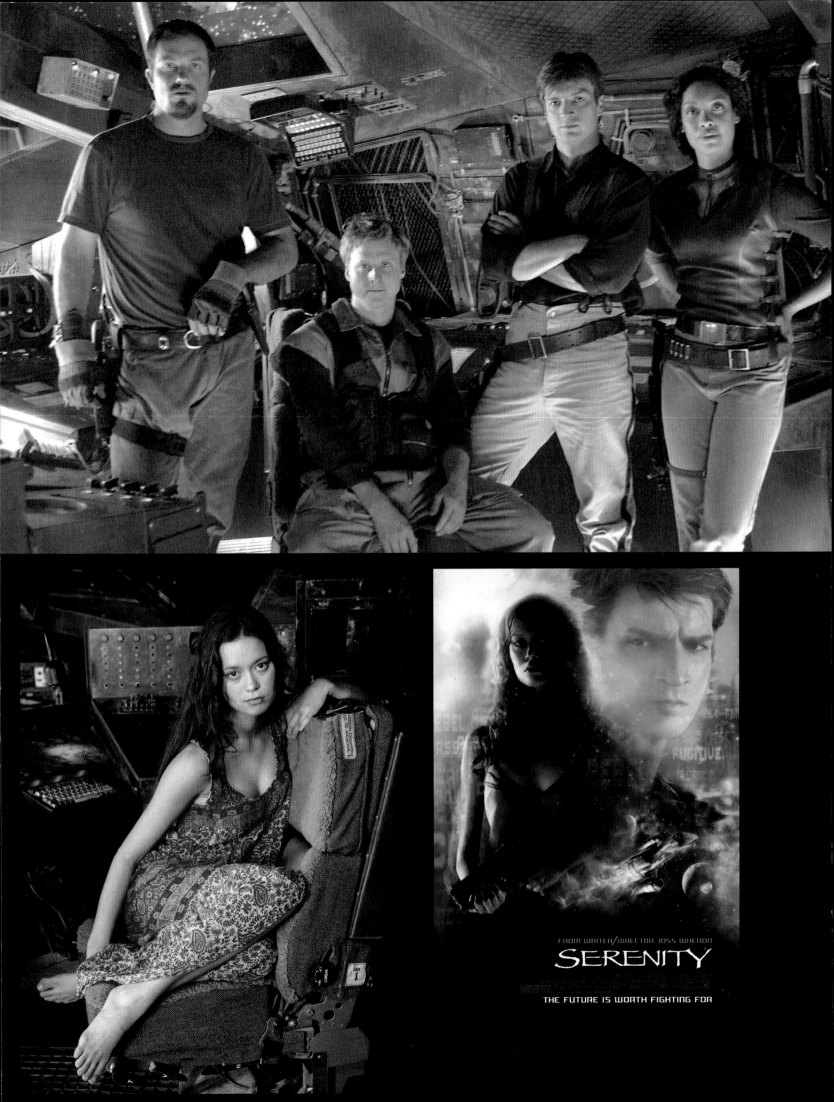

FROM WRITER/DIRECTOR JOSS WHEDON

# SERENITY

THE FUTURE IS WORTH FIGHTING FOR

mechanic; and Dr. Simon Tam (Sean Maher), a physician who is wanted by the Alliance for facilitating the escape of his sister River Tam (Summer Glau), a psychic teenaged prodigy who was the victim of Alliance programming experiments. The *Serenity* earns its keep as a cargo and transport ship—though smuggling and the occasional bank robbery is not out of the question—and its activities bring it into contact with a variety of characters located on distant planets and moons.

Firefly's visual effects received both a Primetime Emmy Award and a Visual Effects Society Award, but the show itself was unable to earn more than a small, if devoted, following. Fox cancelled the show before the end of the first season, and despite a letter-writing campaign and other viewer activism, fans were unable to save the series. That said, *Firefly*'s cult status encouraged Whedon to expand on the story for a theatrical feature, *Serenity*, which he wrote and directed. The 2005 film brought back the television cast and starts by retelling the story of River Tam from *Firefly* and how she was smuggled aboard the *Serenity* by her brother. Because she may be carrying information damaging to the Alliance, they pursue her, landing the ship back into the battle. The expansion from TV to film generated quite a bit of press at the time, but not quite enough to make *Serenity* successful at the box office. Those who loved it in the theaters were still that same small, outlaw band of devotees who had loved it on TV.

### I, Robot

***"You cannot be trusted with your own survival."***

*I, Robot* (2004) is not so much based on the collection of stories by science and sci-fi writer Isaac Asimov, from which the film draws its name, as it is on Asimov's three laws of robotics: (1) robots cannot harm humans, nor allow their inaction to cause harm; (2) robots must follow human orders, unless the order breaks law 1; and (3) a robot must protect its own existence, as long as such protection does not break laws 1 or 2.

The film is set in Chicago in the year 2035, a time when robots are commonplace as menials, workers, and assistants. Detective Del Spooner (Will Smith) is assigned to investigate the suicide of a robotics executive named Lanning. A technophobe despite having a robotic replacement arm, Spooner begins to suspect that Lanning was actually murdered, and by his robot Sonny—a direct violation of the first law. Far worse in terms of lawbreaking follows as robots, spurred on by powerful supercomputer VIKI, begin taking over. It is eventually revealed that VIKI is actually not breaking the three laws of robotics but has logically decided that the human race is destroying itself, and so a robot takeover would actually save human lives. Ultimately VIKI is thwarted, and Spooner realizes that Lanning asked Sonny to kill him so there would be an investigation and VIKI's plan would be detected.

*Above: Detective Spooner (Will Smith) discovers not all robots are created equal in* I, Robot, *based on an Isaac Asimov title.*

*Opposite top: The* Serenity *was called a "firefly class" spaceship because it vaguely resembled a lightning bug.*

*Opposite bottom: Joss Whedon directing Nathan Fillion, Adam Baldwin, and Summer Glau on the set of* Serenity.

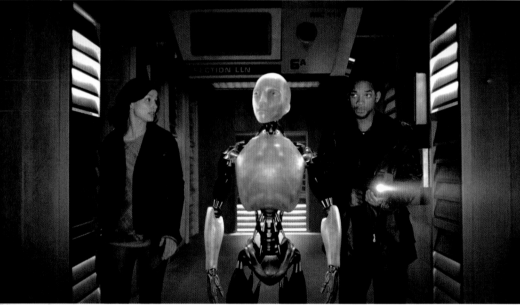

**Above**: In I, Robot, Sonny was animated, but based on recorded performance data from actor Alan Tudyk.

**Left**: Bridget Moynahan and Will Smith flank Sonny in I, Robot.

**Below**: Technophobe Spooner (Will Smith) scowls and bears having to deal with Sonny in I, Robot.

Actor Alan Tudyk provided the performance for Sonny, which was digitally captured and animated by artists at Digital Domain. Much of the action was filmed against a green screen, but a special camera called an Endocam composited the actual set on the sound-stage and the computer-generated set in real time, so that the actors and director Alex Proyas knew what the final result would look like.

*I, Robot* might hold the record for the length of time it took to finally make it onto the screen. Producer John Mantley, best known for TV's *Gunsmoke*, optioned the rights to Asimov's book in 1969 and sold them to Warner Bros. under the assumption that he would produce the film. The studio, however, only wanted the rights and not Mantley, which ended up in a lawsuit that was not settled until 1991, in Mantley's favor. In the meantime, a new script was written by Harlan Ellison that was scheduled to go into production in 1980 with Irwin Kershner, fresh from *The Empire Strikes Back*. Kershner dropped out and was replaced by Ted Kocheff, but the film was scrapped. The script for the film that finally did come out had its roots in an earlier screenplay by Jeff Vintar, which had no connection to Asimov's stories but was instead a murder mystery in which the suspects were all machines. Once the rules of robotics had been attached to it, as well as the familiar title, and the script was rewritten by Hillary Seitz and Akiva Goldman, production of *I, Robot* was finally greenlit with a budget of $120 million. Maybe it would have gone more smoothly if robots had been in charge.

### Eureka

*"Time is unraveling. The laws of physics are breaking down. Correct me if I'm wrong but that's the kind of thing that's not gonna stop at the city limits, is it?"*

Years after returning to private citizenship, President Harry S. Truman told a biographer that setting up the CIA in 1947 was a mistake. "If I'd known what was going to happen," he said, "I never would have done it." In the mythology of the hit Syfy series *Eureka*, Truman also established a top-secret village around a former military base, an idyllic location where the nation's most brilliant scientists can live in peace and work with unlimited resources on scientific and technological advancements that would benefit mankind. Had Truman only known how often things were going to spin out of control there, he might have regretted that one, too.

Eureka, Oregon, cannot be found on any map. Its resident geniuses work for an organization called Global Dynamics, and while their combined achievements have resulted in many of the major technological advancements that everyone uses, there have also been some spectacular flops that no one outside of Eureka knows about. Jack Carter (Colin Ferguson), a U.S. marshal, chances upon the town after having a car accident while transporting his fugitive daughter Zoe (Jordan Hinson) to Los Angeles. This appearance was fortuitous (at least for the off-kilter town), since he is persuaded to become sheriff. Jack finds he is able to keep the peace while investigating some of the strange goings-on that occur in Eureka: everything from the appearance of killer Egyptian scarabs to an epidemic of people turning to stone to being thrust into an entire alternate reality (through the machinations of a one-time associate of Albert Einstein, no less).

***Top***: *Jack Carter (Colin Ferguson, left) finds an ally in Dr. Henry Deacon (Joe Morton) in the odd little town of* Eureka.

***Above***: *Dr. Allison Blake (Salli Richardson-Whitfield) is the government's point person for the goings-on in* Eureka.

**Above**: Deacon and Carter have averted crisis in Eureka . . . maybe.

**Left**: It's time to relax in Eureka.

In between striving to keep the resident scientists from accidentally destroying the world in pursuit of their research, Jack works toward rebuilding his relationship with his daughter, who has a genius IQ herself despite her rebelliousness. Working in tandem to clean up the messes in the town is Dr. Allison Blake (Salli Richardson-Whitfield), Eureka's liaison with the Department of Defense.

Created by Andrew Cosby and Jaime Paglia, the seriocomic series was filmed in Vancouver, with the picturesque town of Chilliwack, British Columbia, standing in for down-town Eureka. Premiering in 2006, it became one of the most successful original series in the history of Syfy, and even aired a partially animated episode for Christmas 2011.

### Transformers
#### *"Before time began, there was the Cube."*
A mysterious object from outer space has landed on Earth. It is a cube covered with glyphs known as the AllSpark, and it is sought by both good aliens called Autobots, led by Optimus Prime, and malicious aliens called Decepticons, led by Megatron. The war between these two has destroyed their home planet, Cybertron, and now Optimus Prime wants the AllSpark to rebuild Cybertron while Megatron wants it to take over the universe. (The AllSpark was discovered by earthlings during the Herbert Hoover administration and concealed by the construction of Hoover Dam.) They continue their galactic battle on Earth, with the Autobots (who can transform into vehicles) aided by young Sam Witwicky (Shia LaBeouf), whose ancestor found the clues leading to the discovery of the AllSpark more than a century earlier.

Directed by Michael Bay, *Transformers* (2007) was based on a wildly popular line of Japanese toys from the 1980s—toys that were fondly remembered by the film's executive producer, Steven Spielberg. "I'd play with them at home with my kids," Spielberg said, "but I'm the one who was enthralled with them." Industrial Light and Magic handled the digital animation of the Transformers and their transformations into vehicles and machinery, requiring up to thirty-eight hours to render one frame of movement. But not every effect was digital. For the climactic scene in which the Decepticon named Bonecrusher blasts through a bus on the freeway, the running Transformer was obviously animated, but the bus was real. It was rigged to explode and separate while four camera cars ran in front and alongside it. The scene was filmed on a section of Interstate 210 near San Bernardino, where the freeway sits uncompleted.

Since the dialogue scenes required the actors to be speaking with gigantic robots that weren't really there, the crew established focal points for the actors to look at by using an extension pole that reached to twenty feet for the Autobot Bumblebee, and forty feet for Optimus Prime.

**Top**: *Bonecrusher blasts through the traffic in* Transformers.

**Above**: *Megan Fox and Shia LaBeouf were the flesh-and-blood stars of* Transformers.

**Top**: *Bonecrusher squares off against Optimus Prime in* Transformers.

**Above middle**: *It's hard to tell the Transformers apart without a program: this one, wiping out the cars, is Starscream.*

**Above**: *The malignant Megatron, from* Transformers.

The end of *Transformers* saw the AllSpark destroyed, Megatron defeated, and the Autobots living in peace on Earth . . . but not for long. Given the enormous success of the film, a sequel was all but assured. In 2009's *Transformers: Revenge of the Fallen*, the primary antagonist was the former Megatronus Prime (also known as "the Fallen"), who actually organized the Decepticons on Earth back during the time of ancient Egypt. Megatron (but not the Fallen) returned for the trilogy's third entry, *Transformers: Dark Side of the Moon* (2011), which opened with the intriguing premise that the U.S. Apollo mission was mandated by President John F. Kennedy to investigate the crash of a Cybertronian spacecraft on the far side of the moon! The Autobots—who are now working with the U.S. government as global peacekeepers—find artifacts left on the moon that renew the battle with the Decepticons.

*Transformers: Dark Side of the Moon* was the first film in the series to achieve more than one *billion* dollars at the box office.

### Cloverfield

**"Approximately seven hours ago, something attacked the city. . . . If you're watching this right now, then you probably know more about it than I do."**

The basic premise of an enormous creature—either of alien origin or enlarged to monstrous proportions through radioactivity—that reduces a major city to rubble has been a staple of science fiction filmmaking for some sixty years. But 2008's *Cloverfield*, in which New York comes under siege by . . . something . . . was unlike any other sci-fi movie before it. The entire film, which focuses on a group of people desperately trying to navigate the city as it is being torn down around them by a largely unseen force, was filmed to look as if it was being recorded on amateur video and phone cameras, entirely through the characters' points of view.

*Cloverfield*'s producer, J. J. Abrams, summed up the film as "a Cameron Crowe movie meets *Godzilla* meets *The Blair Witch Project*." Most giant monster movies, particularly those involving men in creature suits stomping miniature sets, had been shot from "God's point of view," with the camera looking down on the destruction as though it were perched on a cloud. What intrigued Abrams was the thought of people on the ground, looking up and catching only quick glimpses of the thing that is wrecking the city.

Making the shaky cell-phone photography look spontaneous, however, took immense planning on the part of director Matt Reeves and the cast of non-stars (including Michael Stahl-David, Mike Vogel, and Odette Yustman), who filmed much of the footage themselves, in character. Actor T.J. Miller, who played Hud in the film, joked that he shot so much usable footage that he should be allowed to join the cinematographer's union. The unidentified creature was created by Tippett Studios, and was only clearly seen in one shot toward the end. Similarly, the creature's arrival on Earth is seen at the very end of the film, virtually subliminally, in a flashback video that shows a meteor-like object falling into the ocean in the distance. To heighten the reality of the action, *Cloverfield* contains no musical score, only ambient music heard by the characters in the context of the scene.

**Top**: *Rob (Michael Stahl-David) and Beth (Odette Yustman) record themselves in* Cloverfield. *The entire film was made to look like it was shot on personal video.*

**Above**: *Escape from what's left of New York: Jessica Lucas, Michael Stahl-David, and Odette Yustman in* Cloverfield.

**Above**: At the start of Cloverfield, *Rob parties like there's no tomorrow. He's almost right.*

**Right**: *The Statue of Liberty, decapitated by the monster in* Cloverfield.

**Below**: *Even though it looks small, the makers of* Cloverfield *were careful to get the exact right scale for Lady Liberty's severed head.*

**Above**: Joanne Kelly, Saul Rubinek, Allison Scagliotti, and Eddie McClintock in Warehouse 13.

As to why the film is titled *Cloverfield*, which has nothing to do with the action or set-ting, it turns out that Cloverfield Boulevard in West Los Angeles was near Abrams's office, and it became the code name for the film during development. Once news of the project leaked out, the name stuck. In 2011, Abrams would team up with Steven Spielberg for another film whose plot relied heavily on home-shot footage, *Super 8*, a throwback to the likes of *E.T. the Extra-Terrestrial*, about a group of kids filming a movie who discover an alien robot and a government plot to sequester it.

### Warehouse 13
### *"Do you smell fudge in places where there is no fudge?"*

Somewhere in the wilds of South Dakota is Warehouse 13, the repository of supernatu-rally charged artifacts that have belonged to, been used by, or been infused with the linger-ing powers of famous, infamous, and notorious figures of history or legend. The problem is, these objects continue to have an effect on anyone who comes in contact with them, which is why any new ones that turn up have to be hunted down, neutralized, and then carefully stored in the warehouse. And therein lies the chase.

The field agents responsible for tracking these often dangerous objects are Pete Lattimer (Eddie McClintock), a former U.S. Marine with sensitivity to "vibes" and a playful streak, and Myka Bering (Joanne Kelly), a more serious-minded slave to detail. Their obses-sive boss, Artie Nielsen (Saul Rubinek), who sends them on their assignments, is private to the point of being somewhat mysterious yet distrusts technology—he communicates with Lattimer and Bering in the field through a peculiar and not always reliable steampunkish Skype-like device. Handling the high-tech element for the group is the very young Claudia Donovan (Allison Scagliotti), a self-taught wonk who can hack into anything, and housing them—literally—is Leena (Genelle Williams), the aura-sensitive owner of the bed-and-breakfast where the agents live. Overseeing the Warehouse operation is the shadowy Irene Fredric (CCH Pounder), who is Artie's boss, and the liaison with the Warehouse's controlling Regents.

The artifacts that have appeared over the course of the series range from such mun-dane items as combs (Marilyn Monroe's automatically bleaches one's hair, while Lucrezia Borgia's summons up her spirit, which overtakes the user) to the mystical (a deadly Minoan trident) to the downright goofy (Rudolph the Red-Nosed Reindeer's red nose). In the course of their adventures, the team repeatedly comes into contact with the time-jumping H. G. Wells, but not the one of record. This Wells is Helena (played by Jaime Murray), and is the

**Above**: *Agent Pete Lattimer (Eddie McClintock) and Special Agent Artie Nielsen (Saul Rubinek) have their work cut out for them maintaining* Warehouse 13.

**Above right**: *Artie (Saul Rubinek) with one of the bizarre devices found in* Warehouse 13.

**Opposite top**: *Elaborate motion capture of actor Sam Worthington was used to create his Na'vi form in* Avatar.

**Opposite bottom**: *Avatar won 2009 Oscars for Cinematography, Visual Effects, and Art Direction, all of which are represented in this scene.*

sister of the author who has come to be known as H. G. Wells. Before time-traveling into the twenty-first century, Wells was an agent for Warehouse 12, which existed in Victorian England. In the mythology of *Warehouse 13*, it is Helena's bizarre adventures that have been written in books by her brother, who in the series is referred to as "Charles," not "Herbert George." (For the record, the first-recorded warehouse, according to the series' mythology, was built by Alexander the Great.)

Warehouse 13's whimsical approach to action and adventure made the show a hit right out of the gate: its premiere on Syfy in July 2009, written by Brent Mote, Jane Espenson, and David Simkins, scored the highest ratings for any cable program on that particular night. In addition to becoming one of the network's biggest hit series, *Warehouse 13* has served as a crossover nexus point for Syfy's other hit shows, *Eureka* and *Alphas*. A spin-off ten-chapter webisode titled *Warehouse 13: Of Monsters and Men*, launched on Syfy.com in 2011.

### Avatar
**"Up ahead was Pandora. You grew up hearing about it, but I never figured I'd be going there."**

Telling a basic, human story against the backdrop of an unusual or alien world has long been the modus operandi of James Cameron, the Georges Méliès of his day. (Or is the reverse true?) Having pushed the edge of the special effects envelope to tell an underwater adventure tale in *The Abyss* (1989), he shoved it even further to mount a production of *Romeo and Juliet* on board the world's most famous shipwreck in *Titanic* (1997). Then Cameron set every movie record there is in 2009 with *Avatar*, which is essentially an allegory for the European conquest of the Americas set to jaw-dropping imagery. "I wanted to create a familiar type of adventure in an unfamiliar environment," Cameron said at the film's release. He succeeded.

The film is set in 2148 and takes place on Pandora, a moon of the planet Polyphemus in the Alpha Centauri A system. It is a world where an evil corporate entity is mining the mineral "unobtanium," which can solve the problem of Earth's rapidly depleting resources. Avatars, genetically engineered hybrids of human and Na'vi DNA, are more amenable to the planet than humans, who cannot survive on the planet's surface for long. Neytiri (Zoe Saldana) is a Na'vi who takes in human Jake Sully (Sam Worthington), who is relegated to a wheelchair in real life but powerful in Avatar form. Before you can say "Pocahontas," Neytiri and Sully fall in love. Sully fights on behalf of the Na'vis, and when the Earth people are expelled from Pandora, he remains.

Above: Sam Worthington and Zoe Saldana, digitally transformed, in Avatar.

Left: Warrior Tsu'tey (Laz Alonzo) ready for battle in Avatar.

Below: The role of Neytiri in Avatar made actress Zoe Saldana a major star without her ever being seen undigitized.

*Left: Having battled creatures in the Alien franchise, Sigourney Weaver (center) had a much less combative role in Avatar.*

Filmed in 3-D, *Avatar* was, by Cameron's estimation, about 60 percent animated and 40 percent live action. The live—or at least undigitized—cast included Stephen Lang, Sigourney Weaver, and Michelle Rodriguez. The azure-hued, digitally rendered Na'vi, played by Saldana (who parlayed this performance into genuine stardom), CCH Pounder, Wes Studi, and Laz Alonso, were created via performance-capture technology, in which an actor's performance is data-recorded to inform the computer animation. But the motion capture used for *Avatar* was done at six times the capacity usually employed for visual effects. Head rigs were developed that were capable of capturing every nuance of facial expression, even when projected on an IMAX-sized screen. Cameron had conceptualized *Avatar* in 1995 but put it aside until the photorealistic capability of digital animation caught up with what he envisioned in his head. It was worth the wait, since despite its $237 million price tag, *Avatar* has become the most profitable movie in history, grossing, as of this writing, $2.78 *billion* worldwide, and was one of the rare sci-fi films to be nominated for an Academy Award as Best Picture. Cameron has stated that he plans to make two sequels to the film.

### District 9
*"You are not welcome here."*

In the early 1980s, a large spaceship appears over Johannesburg, South Africa, and inside are a race of clearly ailing, exoskeletal aliens. They are brought down to Earth, where they are dismissively referred to as "prawns" and housed in a ramshackle camp called District 9. A corporation called MultiNational Unlimited (MNU) has been engaged by the government to move all the aliens out of District 9 and into a new camp. But MNU is far less interested in the aliens than they are in their technology and weapons, which will only work when activated by alien DNA. When one MNU field agent named Wikus van der Merwe (Sharlton Copley) gets an alien virus that alters his DNA, he suddenly becomes invaluable, since his DNA can be used to activate the alien technology. To avoid vivisection by his superiors, who want the secrets of his DNA, Wikus escapes into District 9. There he is taken in by a sympathetic alien named Christopher Johnson, whom Wikus agrees to help obtain a canister of the substance that made Wikus ill, and which can also be used to reactivate

the spaceship. Christopher ends up taking off for his home planet but promises to return in three years. Wikus, however, fully transforms into a prawn, but he still retains his human memories.

Produced by Peter Jackson, *District 9* (2009) was co-written and directed by Neill Blomkamp, who based it on an earlier short film called *Alive in Joburg*. Many critics saw the aliens in camps as a metaphor for apartheid, but Blomkamp claimed there was no metaphoric message in the film despite its dark satire. The film was made to look like a mockumentary, with three points of view: the action, which looks like documentary, handheld footage; actual news footage, gleaned from the South African Broadcasting Corporation and Reuters; and a corporate video for MNU, which offers exposition.

The "prawns" were designed by artists at Jackson's Weta Digital in New Zealand, but the studio was too swamped with work for *Avatar* to execute the effects. That was left to Vancouver-based Imagine Engine. The setting of District 9 itself was a genuine impoverished urban area called Tshiawelo, which is in Soweto, near Johannesburg. Echoing the plot of the film, the township had recently been inhabited but the residents were being moved to government housing. The film unit took over the shantytown and rebuilt some of the shacks with the junk left behind.

Much of the dialogue for the film was improvised, using a privately produced graphic novel as a story guide. Only about ten copies of the graphic novel were printed, and none were released commercially, though it was also used to secure financing. The movie was picked up by Sony, and given a successful viral marketing campaign that was launched at San Diego Comic-Con, one of the premier genre conventions in the world, which caters to more than one hundred thousand attendees each summer. *District 9* proved to be a hit everywhere except Nigeria, which banned the film for its depiction of Nigerians as criminals, and in one instance, a bloodthirsty cannibal.

*Top*: Wikus van der Merwe (Sharlto Copley) deals with a "prawn" in District 9.

*Above*: Contact with the alien virus turns Wikus from a government ally to a wanted man in District 9.

*Opposite top*: The alien spaceship remains fixed over South Africa for decades in District 9.

*Opposite below*: Actor Sharlto Copley (foreground) improvised most of his dialogue for District 9.

**Left**: Dr. Lee Rosen (David Strathairn) leads the Alphas team.

**Below**: Malik Yoba, Azita Ghanizada, and David Strathairn in Syfy's Alphas.

**Opposite top**: David Strathairn and Azita Ghanizada in Alphas.

**Opposite bottom**: The stories of Alphas tend to give more weight to crime investigations than to special effects and super heroics.

## Alphas
### *"Impossible is what they do best."*

If the Impossible Missions Force from *Mission: Impossible* had all been blessed with heightened physical and mental powers, they might have become the team from *Alphas*, which premiered on Syfy in 2011. Created by Zak Penn, whose screenwriting résumé includes the superhero films *The Avengers*, *The Incredible Hulk*, and *X-Men: The Last Stand*, *Alphas* is about a group of five outwardly ordinary young people—they don't transform into anything or even wear skintight leotards (though they'd look good in them if they did)—who have heightened senses and abilities.

Gary (Ryan Cartwright) has a brain like a computer and the ability to visualize electromagnetic impulses; Rachel (Azita Ghanizada) can hyper-intensify one sense at a time by short-circuiting the other four; Cameron (Warren Christie), a former U.S. Marine sharpshooter, can gauge movement at superhuman speed and thus eyeball a bullet's trajectory; Bill (Malik Yoba), an ex-FBI agent, has an adrenaline level that can hit instantly and like a tsunami, giving him brief bursts of unnatural strength; and Nina (Laura Menell) can control people's actions with her mind. The twist is that the powers also come with downsides; Bill's adrenalin rush, for instance, gives him anger management issues, while the price for Gary possessing his computer brain is autism. Still, under the leadership of brain scientist Dr. Lee Rosen (David Strathairn), the group works for the Department of Defense to investigate crimes perpetrated by other Alphas who are controlled by an organization called Red Flag.

Shot in Toronto, which stands in for the show's New York setting, *Alphas*, which premiered on Syfy in the summer of 2011, is structured as an adventure/crime drama with action and special effects. *Alphas* has also become part of the interconnected Syfy universe, through the appearance of *Warehouse 13* character Dr. Vanessa Calder (Lindsay Wagner) in the first-season episode "Never Let Me Go." "Alphas," by the way, should not be confused with the "Abnormals," which are the sometimes mythological, occasionally monstrous—but real—entities that are the focus of the weekly Syfy series *Sanctuary*.

**Above**: *Hugo (Asa Butterfield) and Isabelle (Chloë Grace Moretz) with the mechanical mystery that is at the center of* Hugo.

**Opposite**: *Cinema pioneer Georges Méliès (Ben Kingsley) discovers he is not as forgotten as he assumed in* Hugo.

## Hugo

*"If you ever wonder where your dreams come from, look around you: this is where they're made."*

An old, embittered man sells mechanical toys out of a booth in a Paris train station in the 1930s; a young orphan to whom it has fallen, through a series of misfortunes, the responsibility of keeping the clocks in the train station running, tries to steal parts from the toy seller to fix a wondrous mechanical windup man who, when operational, will write on paper. For the boy, Hugo Cabret (Asa Butterfield), the mechanical man is all he has left of his late father, who found the contraption rusting in a museum and brought it home to fix. Hugo is convinced that his father left a message for him that will be revealed through the automaton's writing but is unable to get it to work fully because it requires a special heart-shaped key to wind it.

Man and boy are thrust together, and it turns out that the key belongs to the old toy maker's goddaughter Isabelle (Chloë Grace Moretz), an adventurous girl who wants to help Hugo solve the mystery. Once properly wound, the automaton draws a fanciful picture of a space capsule hitting the face of the moon, and signs the drawing "Georges Méliès" . . . the name of her godfather, the old toy maker, who built the automaton years earlier!

Based on the children's book *The Invention of Hugo Cabret*, by Brian Selznick, *Hugo* (2011) presents a fictional version of the final years of the great pioneering filmmaker's life, three decades after *A Trip to the Moon*, during which time Méliès was reduced to selling toys in a Paris train station. Méliès was rediscovered by film buffs of the 1930s, but it took one of the film industry's most fervent film buffs, director Martin Scorsese, to put Méliès's story up on the big screen. Sir Ben Kingsley plays the legendary filmmaker, and so closely resembled the real man that actual footage of Méliès in his prime was intercut with the actor, with convincing results.

Originally, animation director Chris Wedge (*Ice Age*; *Robots*) was attached to the film as director (and the film's simple story structure, cartoony supporting characters, camera acrobatics, and stylized digital Paris cityscapes make the film *look* like a live-action animated feature), but then-producer Graham King suggested it to Scorsese, with whom he had made *The Departed*. What resonated with Scorsese about the project was its connection to the birth of cinema. What also captivated the director was the opportunity to shoot the film in 3-D, so much so that he specifically cast a Doberman pinscher as the "bloodhound" of the train-station policeman in order to take full stereoscopic advantages of its long nose in 3-D! The film's elaborate, evocative re-creation of the Paris train station was constructed on the back lots of Shepperton and Longcross studios in England, taking six months to build. Much of the action, though, was filmed on location in Paris.

Best of all, *Hugo* contains clips of several of Méliès's films, many resplendent in their original hand-tinted color, reminding modern audiences why Georges Méliès deserves the title of the Father of Sci-Fi Cinema.

## Appendix

Time and space, of course, preclude discussing every notable science fiction movie or television show ever made—or even the majority of them. The list below contains one hundred additional films and programs that are not discussed within these pages, but which would be of interest to any sci-fi fan.

### Films

The Lost World (1925)
The Mysterious Island (1929)
Dr. Jekyll and Mr. Hyde (1931)
Frankenstein (1931)
The Invisible Man (1933)
The Island of Lost Souls (1933)
The Invisible Ray (1936)
Man-Made Monster (1941)
Haredevil Hare (cartoon; 1948)
Donovan's Brain (1953)
Duck Dodgers in the 24½th Century (cartoon; 1953)
Invaders from Mars (1953)
It Came from Outer Space (1953)
Red Planet Mars (1953)
The Creeping Unknown (a.k.a. The Quatermass Xperiment; 1955)
Earth vs. The Flying Saucers (1956)
Not of This Earth (1957)
The Amazing Colossal Man (1957)
The Blob (1958)
The Colossus of New York (1958)
I Married a Monster from Outer Space (1958)
The Incredible Shrinking Man (1958)
On the Beach (1959)
The Lost World (1960)
Voyage to the Bottom of the Sea (1961)
The Day of the Triffids (1962)
X: The Man with X-Ray Eyes (1963)
The Time Travelers (1964)
Crack in the World (1965)
Seconds (1966)
Five Million Miles to Earth (a.k.a. Quatermass and the Pit; 1967)
The Power (1968)
Journey to the Far Side of the Sun (1969)
Marooned (1969)
Colossus: The Forbin Project (1970)
A Clockwork Orange (1971)
Slaughterhouse Five (1972)
Fantastic Planet (1973)
Sleeper (1973)
Dark Star (1974)
Zardoz (1974)
The Rocky Horror Picture Show (1975)
The Stepford Wives (1975)
Wizards (1977)
The Black Hole (1979)
Altered States (1980)
Escape from New York (1981)
Heavy Metal (1981)
Time Bandits (1981)
Brazil (1985)
Lifeforce (1985)

Little Shop of Horrors (1986)
Innerspace (1987)
Predator (1987)
The Running Man (1987)
Akira (1988)
Honey, I Shrunk the Kids (1989)
The Handmaid's Tale (1990)
The Rocketeer (1990)
Timecop (1994)
Ghost in the Shell (1995)
Species (1995)
12 Monkeys (1995)
Independence Day (1996)
Mars Attacks! (1996)
Starship Troopers (1997)
Armageddon (1998)
Dark City (1998)
Galaxy Quest (1999)
Mission to Mars (2000)
Titan A.E. (2000)
A.I. Artificial Intelligence (2001)
Equilibrium (2002)
Minority Report (2002)
Idiocracy (2006)
V for Vendetta (2007)
I Am Legend (2008)
WALL-E (2008)
The Book of Eli (2010)
Battle: Los Angeles (2011)
Cowboys and Aliens (2011)

### Television

Out There (1951–52)
Tales of Tomorrow (1951–53)
Science Fiction Theatre (1955–57)
Supercar (1961–62)
Fireball XL5 (1962–63)
The Jetsons (1962–63)
Thunderbirds (1965–66)
It's About Time (1966–67)
Captain Nice (1967)
Mr. Terrific (1967)
Space: 1999 (1975–78)
Blake's 7 (1978–81)
The Martian Chronicles (miniseries; 1980)
The Hitchhiker's Guide to the Galaxy (miniseries; 1981)
Amazing Stories (1985–87)
seaQuest DSV (1993–96)
Futurama (1999–)
Dune (miniseries; 2000)
Fringe (2008–)

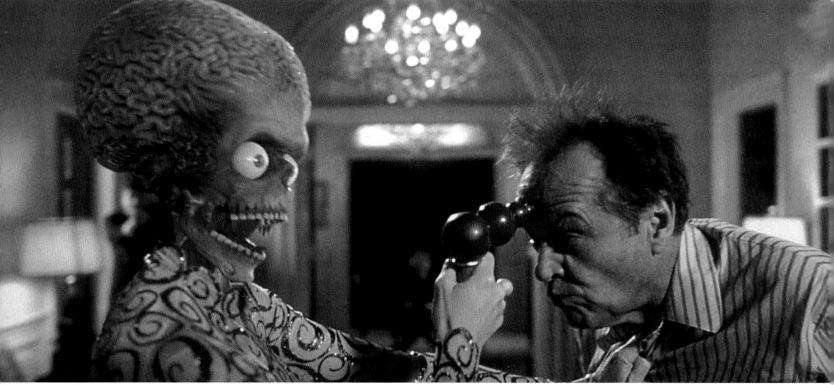

**Top**: *Chuck Jones' Duck Dodgers in the 24th ½ Century (1953) was the third cartoon to feature Marvin the Martian, but arguably the most memorable.*

**Above**: *The President (Jack Nicholson) is about to get zapped by a barely-disguised Martian in Mars Attacks!, probably the best film to have been based on a series of trading cards. Seriously.*

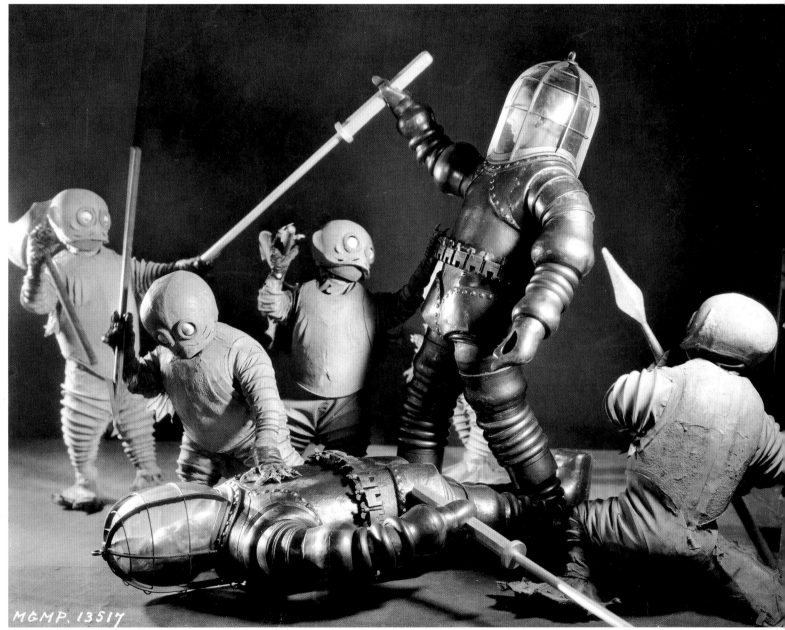

MGMP. 13517

**Top**: Robots to the rescue in 2008's animated view of the future, WALL-E.

**Above**: The 1929 adaptation of Jules Verne's The Mysterious Island had only a few talkie sequences, but was filmed in Technicolor. The strange little creatures seen here are supposed to be part of an underwater race.

THE SCIENCE FICTION UNIVERSE . . . AND BEYOND

*Above*: Special effects such as those that put Grant Williams in conflict with a gigantic cat highlighted 1957's The Incredible Shrinking Man.

**Top**: *Who says you can't fight Washington? The aliens mean business in 1996's Independence Day.*

**Above**: *Keep watching the skies!*

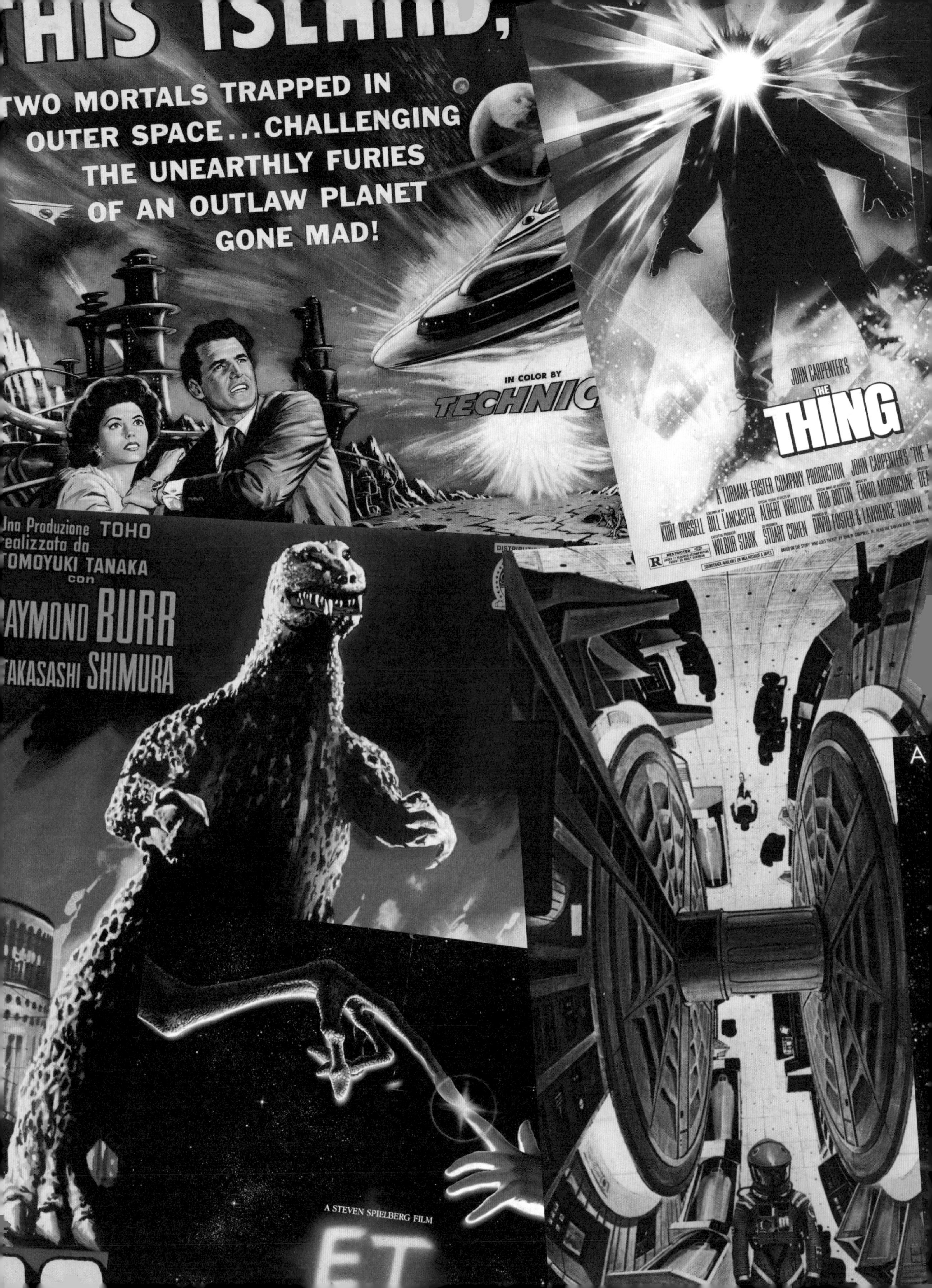